To Billy

Even super [illegible]
also manage personalities

Best Wishes

Barney

MANAGE THE PERSONALITY NOT THE PERSON

by

R.R.BAXTER and CLYDE L. ROUSEY

Graphics by Kath Howell

Published by Baxter Associates, Inc.

Suite 503

1250 West Northwest Highway

Palatine,IL 60067

Phone: 847.359.5599, Fax: 847.359.5874

E-Mail: rrbaxter@baxter-inc.com

Successful management in an organization is not dependent on gender. Throughout this book we have alternated where possible the pronouns he and she to emphasize this point.

None of the examples used in this book refer to a specific individual living or dead. They represent a composite of our collective experience in application of the ideas we discuss.

Publisher's Cataloging-in-Publication
(Provided by Quality Books, Inc.)

Baxter, R. R.
Manage the personality—not the person / by R. R. Baxter and Clyde L. Rousey; graphics by Kath Howell – 1 st ed.
p. cm.
LCCN: 00-190695
ISBN: 0-615-11135-1

1. Personnel management. 2. Executives - - Psychology. 3. Personality and occupation. 4. Personality assessment. I. Rousey, Clyde L. II. Title

HF5549.B39 2000 658.407
QB100-506

CONTENTS

TRANSFORMATION PARTICIPANTS

MISCELLANEOUS TRANSFORMATION ISSUES

PERSONALITY ISSUES

APPENDIX

ACKNOWLEDGEMENTS

Were it not for the patient and efficient handling of both the early and final drafts by Karen Sleeman we would never have had material to hand to our other consultants. The graphic work for the cover of this book reflects the unique style and capability of Janice Hansen. The illustrations found throughout this book as well as on the cover are original contributions by Kath Howell.

We have appreciated the technical support provided by Barker Printing. Anne Francis, Ph.D., Jack Fitzpatrick, Ph.D. and David Morrison, M.D provided early reading of our book with helpful comments.

Finally, we thank Jameson Baxter, President of the Baxter Investment Group and Carol Rousey, Ph.D. who in addition to their "personal affiliation" with the authors also provided perceptive and critical suggestions. Such help is most useful and can only come from persons who are close.

PREFACE

We wrote this book to describe a new management technique for both experienced and new managers. It is based on the 40+ years of practical experience by Baxter and his 20+ years of acquaintance with and practical application of some of the psychological concepts of the co-author.

There is a great deal of overlap between sound psychological principles and sound principles of management. The two areas have more in common than at first blush might seem possible. Our hope is not to make managers into psychologists or psychologists into managers. Rather, we feel the two disciplines both augment and complement each other and in so doing can enhance the skills of managers as well as the productivity of business. This practical application involves relating personalities and jobs to optimize efficiency and effectiveness in large and small companies and in managing transformation situations.

We feel organizations are in a state of either "crisis or constant transformation". The first 10 chapters discuss and illustrate how personality and emotions are played out at all levels of an organization. Next, we discuss specific management challenges and how personality affects day-to-day decisions. Finally, in the last three chapters, we provide general information about personality factors that we have used in our presentation. The appendix provides a detailed discussion of one approach to assessment and understanding of personality.

Some readers may experience the ideas we present as a new business theory. Yet, as we will demonstrate, many of the concepts we discuss have been available for many years and from many sources. In this regard, we call attention to the pioneering work of Harry Levinson and his colleagues who long ago pointed out how personality is important in successful management. We note that our suggestions for effective management run counter to some of the more cognitive approaches of Peter Drucker, Elliott Jacques and others.

Managers who have a good psychological understanding of themselves can most easily implement the ideas we propose. Trouble in use of the concepts should alert a manager to the possibility that they may have some blind spots in understanding their own emotions. While we do not wish to foreclose any disagreements with our proposals, we do want the reader to be aware that new ideas are sometimes resisted for reasons that have no seeming conscious awareness.

While we provide supplementary reading suggestions which present other views, it is not our intent to provide a treatise which includes experimental research about our assertions. We leave this to academia and to the practical test of management.

Chapter 1

INTRODUCTION

Practical ideas for improving the management skills of top and middle managers and of front-line supervisors have been widely available for some time. Programs that integrate such ideas with known psychological principles and theory are not as readily accessible. This book presents a blueprint to help you recognize and apply these key maxims:

- The personality of an individual is not easily modified and can materially affect his job performance.
- An individual's personality must fit his specific job and be compatible with the personality profile of the group in which he works.
- Failure to take into account the personality profiles of the individual and the group can seriously reduce the effectiveness of even the best-run organization.

An individual's job performance is determined more by his personality and emotional state than by his skill or education. Personality, in the present context, refers to normal variations in personality as opposed to psychopathology. Personality may include both traits and behaviors, but it is not meant to designate a psychiatric diagnosis. As used in this book, the concept of personality refers to unique mental behaviors used by an individual in his relationships with others. These behaviors reflect a mixture of physical and neurological integrity with early, past, and current life experiences.

Management first must decide which personality factors are relevant for a particular position and then match

the personality to the job. A personality profile should be established for each job classification in an organization. If the personality does not fit the job requirements, even though the individual may be brilliant and dedicated, you will not obtain the optimum performance from him. Likewise, if the personality of the individual is not compatible with the personality profile of the group or team with whom he is to work, full success cannot be achieved.

The right people have to be in the right place if they are to effect positive change, to fix problems, or to assure the transformation necessary for the organization. The quality of the individual workers and the match of their personalities to their job requirements are more important in a transformation than the number of people involved.

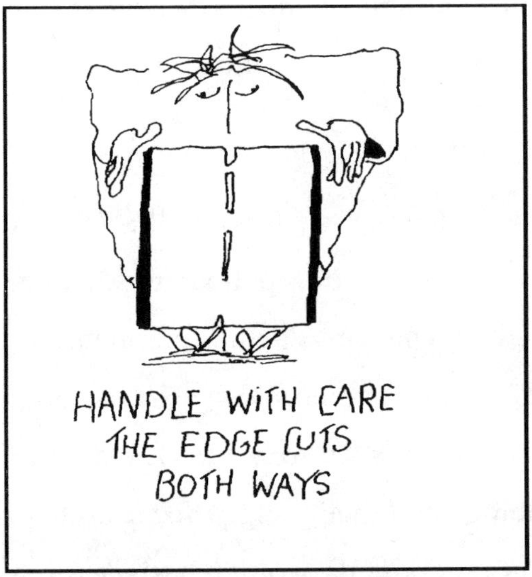

This management approach is not at odds with what many successful industry leaders are doing today. It may be a useful approach for organizations that are not meeting their operational or strategic goals. In most companies experiencing difficulty, you are likely to find serious mismatches between the personalities of the managers in charge and the requirements of the jobs they are expected to perform.

Various authorities have estimated that between 50% and 75% of top managers fail in their jobs. Although some may fail because they lack technical and experiential background, many fail because their personalities are not well matched to their positions. To be successful, a manager must be able to deal with an organization that requires constant transformation and also to manage personalities, not just people.

In the following pages we will show you how these basic assumptions can be applied in situations requiring either immediate change to avoid imminent disaster (*crisis transformation*) or ongoing change in the ordinary course of business (*constant transformation*). We will also discuss how psychological functioning affects both personal and corporate success on a day-to-day basis and how managers can be alert to and address these issues.

Suggested Reading

For other perspectives on the topics discussed in this book the interested reader may wish to also read:

1. Francis, A. (1999). *The daughter also rises*, San Francisco: Rudi Publishing.

2. Goleman, D. (1998). What makes a leader? *Harvard Business Review, 76*, Nov.-Dec., 93-102.

3. Hogan, R., Raskin, R., & Frazzini, D. (1990). The dark side of charisma. In: K. E. Clark and M. B. Clark (Eds.), *Measures of Leadership* (343-354). West Orange, NJ: Leadership Library of America.

4. Jacques, E. & Clement, S. (1991). *Executive leadership*, Arlington, VA: Cason Hall and Co.

5. Jones, J., Steffy, B. & Bray, D. (Eds.). (1991). *Applying psychology in business: Handbook for managers and human resource professionals*. Lexington, MA: Lexington Books, D.C. Heath & Co.

6. Kotter, John P. (1996). *Leading change*. Boston, MA: Harvard Business School Press.

7. Levinson, H. (1994). Why the behemoths fell. *American Psychologist*, 49, 428-436.

8. Levinson, H., & Rosenthal, S. (1984). *CEO.* New York: Basic Books.

9. Millon, T. (1996). *Disorders of Personality: DSM IV and Beyond.* New York: John Wiley & Sons, Inc.

10. Rousey, C., Morrison, D., & Deacon, D. (1995). Choosing successful management. *Consulting Psychology Journal*, 108-113.

Chapter 2

TRANSFORMATIONS

You should consider every day a transformation situation. When you assume leadership in a troubled company, attain a new level of leadership, or replace a manager who has left or been terminated, you are in a transformation situation. There are two basic kinds of transformation: crisis and constant.

CRISIS TRANSFORMATION

Crisis transformation is a short-term, usually one-shot process required to turn around an organization that is at imminent risk of failure. A crisis transformation situation usually means that the corporation is on the verge of Chapter 11 bankruptcy. This situation demands immediate financial as well as managerial attention. For our purposes, the terms ***reengineering*** and ***turnaround*** are synonyms for crisis transformation.

What should you expect to find in a company that requires a major transformation? We wish to underline the idea that **a transformation situation does not necessarily mean downsizing**. Transformation situations come in all sizes, shapes, and forms. A looming Chapter 11 requires a major effort–a crisis transformation. This situation can be addressed easily because it is so obvious. If the troubled organization is to survive, it will require immediate infusions of financial assistance and, more importantly, leadership and managerial assistance.

Who's left? In the obvious transformation situation, you should not expect to find a plethora of capability left in the management and supervisory ranks. Most situations requiring such drastic action do not occur overnight. They result from mismanagement or lack of leadership over a period of time. Constant transformation has not been practiced. Typically, the most capable people have already departed. They long ago saw the handwriting on the wall, perhaps even before management faced up to the reality of the situation. You should expect to find mediocrity in the management ranks. However, occasionally you will find a jewel who has been unable or unwilling, for one reason or another, to leave for a better position.

Review the personality of each individual in the organization and immediately overhaul the structure of the organization. Your primary objective is to realign the personnel to best fit their individual personalities to the clearly defined tasks required to effect the transformation.

CONSTANT TRANSFORMATION

Constant transformation is the process of reacting swiftly to outside data in a proactive and decisive manner to enhance the effectiveness and efficiency of the organization. Constant change becomes the norm. Constant transformation is necessary for an organization to survive today. The organization must continually strive to maintain or improve its position. Only with the knowledge and active

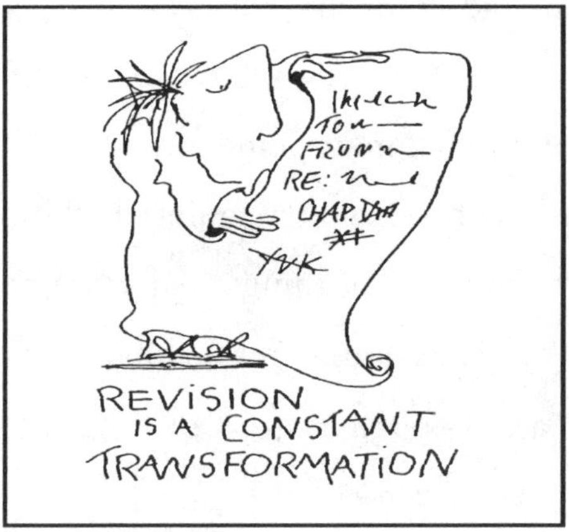

management of personality, not just the person, can management successfully meet this challenge.

Constant transformation differs from ***constant process improvement*** in significant ways. Constant improvement programs are designed to continually improve the process in terms of quality and cost efficiency in order to produce the same base end product or result. The basic process is improved but not structurally changed. Constant transformation continually changes the process structure in reaction to outside data or forces to better meet the market's changing demands. The basic process is changed and improved, and this is a never-ending endeavor.

The need for transformation is not always obvious: When an organization is in a no-growth period (or very slow growth compared to its competition) and the present management of the company believes that performance is satisfactory or is about to be so, the need for transformation is less obvious. In fact, management may even compare the financial ratios with other companies in the same line of business and conclude that things really are not too bad or even that they are doing reasonably well. Whatever business they are in–buggy whips or dot.com, they should not be misled. Their present situation is the precursor to a Chapter 11, only given enough time.

Outside data are critical: Constant transformation is the response of the organization to outside data. The rate of transformation has to equal or exceed the rate of change in the outside data. Otherwise, the organization falls behind the market changes. If the response to the outside data is not corrected in time, then a crisis transformation will be required to return the organization to a position to continue with constant transformation. In other words, the required rate of constant transformation is directly proportional to the rate of change in the outside data. Fall behind, and you will require a crisis transformation.

A company operating in a comfortable mode, although it is not responding proactively to outside data, has not yet deteriorated to the point that the Board of Directors is excited or the shareholders worried. This is the most difficult situation to change because change cannot be initiated until the need for it is recognized. If the management has permitted this situation to continue over a period of time, they certainly are not going to call 911 and jeopardize their comfortable positions.

Sam Walton made the difference: This deceptively comfortable attitude by management apparently led some major companies such as General Motors, International Business Machines (IBM), and Sears, Roebuck & Company into serious financial difficulties during the decade of the 1990s. Sears, in particular, felt that they were in very good shape since their earnings were reasonable and they were still paying dividends. They failed to look over their shoulder to see if anyone was gaining on them; they did not make use of outside data. In fact, not only was someone gaining on them, two someones were gaining on them. K-Mart and Wal-Mart not only gained on Sears, but also passed Sears by. According to the *Wall Street Journal*, November 5, 1993, K-Mart surpassed Sears in sales in 1990 as the number one retailer. Then in January 1991, Wal-Mart took over the top retailing spot from K-Mart. In 1992, with 400 fewer stores, Wal-Mart store sales were 50% higher than K-Mart sales of $26.5 billion. At the end

of 1998, Wal-Mart's net earnings were 8 times those of K-Mart! Once your competition has passed you up, it is virtually impossible to catch up again. A major effort is required to regain momentum. Sam Walton kept Wal-Mart in constant transformation.

"Japan, Inc.," needs repair: American companies are not the only ones who have failed to exercise constant transformation. The March 1, 1999, issue of *Time Magazine* highlighted the problems of NISSAN in its article "Nissan Calls for a Tow."

> HIGH LABOR COSTS–Lifetime job security means Nissan has too many workers, and the *keiretsu* has become a major burden.

> SLOW BOSSES–Consensus-driven management discourages risk-taking. Nissan needs an overhaul.
>
> POOR SALES–Nissan's cars are well made, but the company's designs have not kept up with the marketplace.

Manage the Personality-Not the Person

This is a good example of what can happen to a company in only ten years. Nissan was synonymous with "Japan, Inc.," and was putting the fear into Detroit's' Big Three. What happened? Management failed to respond to outside data. They did not ask the public what they wanted in a car design. Management dictated to the designers what was good for the public. Had Nissan management been students of history, they would have known that Henry Ford did the same thing during the 1920s and almost bankrupted Ford Motor Company. *Time* noted, "Nissan's consensus-driven style and corporate structure may have been acceptable in the go-go 80's, but they don't work well when drastic decisions have to be made quickly." Nissan is now on the acquisition block.

If you remember when the IBM mainframe dominated the computer market, you may also remember that the mantra of the corporate information technologist was "You never get fired for buying Big Blue." IBM owned not only the mainframe market but also the entire computing market. The absence of constant transformation during the explosive growth of the PC reduced IBM to the state of requiring a crisis transformation, which was performed brilliantly by Mr. Louis V. Gretna, Jr. Is there any doubt that constant transformation is now part of the new IBM culture?

If a company is to avoid the Sears/Nissan/IBM syndrome, then it is imperative that the management of the company always operates as if someone were gaining on them. They need to operate in a constant transformation mode.

If you are constantly trying to improve the efficiency and effectiveness of your operation, then there is less need to be looking over your shoulder. You should easily stay ahead of the pack. The physical law of inertia applies in this instance. Once an object is in motion, it tends to remain in motion unless some outside force is applied. Conversely, an object at rest tends to remain at rest.

Management must look upon each and every day as a transformation challenge, whether it is a crisis transformation or the daily activity of an organization in constant transformation. For an organization to become successful or continue to be successful, it should operate every day as if it were in constant transformation. The organization should apply the same energy, the same urgency, the same philosophy, and the same principles in its everyday operations as it would in the midst of a crisis transformation (turnaround) to avoid imminent bankruptcy. Management must push the envelope to just short of chaos; in fact, successfully managed companies do maintain a state of near chaos. If change were managed to and at the edge of chaos, then the continued success and longevity of the organization would be maximized.

In the following chapters, we will identify the key players in any transformation and some of the specific issues that they must manage. We will analyze their roles, their psychological states, and the personality factors that are critical to transformation management. We believe that management by constant transformation can help a company avoid major and painful changes.

Transformation Participants

Chapter 3

BOARDS OF DIRECTORS

THE CORPORATE BOARD

The Board of Directors should set policy for the company, take action to assure the company's perpetuation, monitor the performance of the CEO, and take appropriate action when it does not meet expectations. Liability laws and the courts have broadened the definition of the director's fiduciary responsibility and increased the penalties for not carrying it out in a prudent manner. Board members are becoming more cognizant of the importance of their role.

Expect to find trouble: In a transformation situation, you can expect to find certain things. Some very important things you almost assuredly will not find. It normally takes a company several years to reach such a deplorable financial state that it brings in new management to do a crisis transformation.

Manage the Personality–Not the Person

Expect to find the employees disenchanted with the board. They have known for a long time that their leader is not performing at a competent level. They have talked–and yes, gossiped–wondering when the Board of Directors would finally get smart enough and/or muster the collective will to suggest a better employment opportunity elsewhere for the "ol' boy." Some employees may have formed secret alliances with some board members. The board itself may be split into factions, further complicating communication for management.

Nevertheless, the board will allow the CEO to run the company into Chapter 11, or at least to the courthouse steps, before it acts. The Board of Directors may not replace the CEO in a timely fashion. Their relationship with him may be a "good ol' boys' club." The CEO has hand-picked the members of the board (both inside and outside directors). They won't bite the hand that feeds them unless they are forced to do so. If history is any gauge, the CEO has to be incompetent for a long time before they will even nibble his fingers.

Don't be a mushroom: Many managers treat their board members, particularly the outside directors, like mushrooms. They keep them in the dark and feed them what you feed mushrooms. Board members can never know as much as management. Outside board members should not be deep into the business. That is not their job or responsibility. The board's charge is not to micromanage the company. That is management's responsibility.

Should you be elected a director, don't allow yourself to be treated like a mushroom. Don't act like a mushroom. Move out of the cave and into the light. Act like a real director. Hold the CEO accountable on a timely basis.

Avoid the minefields: When you walk into an organization to replace its CEO, the board will be partly or totally loyal to the departed CEO. After all, the departed CEO appointed them. Step carefully. You will be walking across a minefield.

You will need not only business acumen but also political shrewdness to deal effectively with this situation. Of all the times you need a friendly and helpful board, the most critical is during a crisis transformation. You must put the entire operation into a crisis mode to survive. You need to fight on the main battlefront, rather than defend the rear against unfriendly and non-supportive board members.

For instance, one particular board was composed of nine members--four founders, four venture capitalists and the CEO. The senior author was the CEO. The founders had one set of goals for the company: long-term growth and long-term employment. The venture capitalists had another set: get in, get rich, and get out. The CEO's goals encompassed some of both, plus saving the company, keeping peace on the board, and not surrendering his authority to the board. Conflict inevitably led to attempted micro-management of the company by the venture capitalists on the board. These actions generated an inordinate amount of stress for all parties involved, especially for the CEO. A classic Catch 22 developed for all parties. Watch out for those minefields.

Composition of the board is more important than its size: Unless you have a billion-dollar-plus company, nine directors are too many to manage during a crisis. To manage effectively, you must communicate effectively. In a crisis, communication must be excessive. No one ever over-communicates. The lesser the demand on the communication needs the greater the effort available to concentrate on managing the crisis. The composition of the board is more important than the number.

Beware of the mushrooms: Don't take the turnaround job unless you can be assured of a capable, friendly board that shares your values, your goals for the corporation and your strategy for accomplishing these goals. If you don't settle the board issue before you say yes,

then beware of the attack mushrooms. They will emerge from the cave of darkness. The saying *Once burned, twice cautious* probably originated because of action by the members of the first Board of Directors of the Cavemen's Condominium Association.

THE COOPERATIVE BOARD

Special challenges: The Board of Directors of a cooperative presents a special set of challenges for the Chief Executive Officer. If the organization is a supply cooperative, the board members are and represent your customers. They come with all the expectations and demands of a discriminating buyer, such as best quality, best service and the lowest price! If the organization is a marketing cooperative, the board members will be growers. They come with all the expectations and demands of the discriminating producer or seller, such as outstanding but low cost service and highest product prices.

Conflicts of interest: Cooperative boards by nature of their composition are wrought with built-in conflicts of interest. The best interest of the organization must come before the interest of the entity represented by the board member. This is counter-intuitive. The fiduciary responsibility required of a member of the cooperative board demands a high level of reality testing.

The "Hired Hand": The manager must have a facility for the political, the patience of Job, and the thick skin of the rhino to accept being treated as the "hired-hand." Since the board is composed primarily of farmer/producers who have "hired-hands" on their farms, this familiar treatment carries over to the top management of the cooperative. This attitude is exacerbated further by the fact that the CEO is not a member of the board.

Tyranny of the minority: Cooperative boards work diligently to make decisions by consensus. This trait of governance leads to tyranny of the minority. Compromise requires disproportionate concessions. The CEO must understand and manage the personality of each board member and the politics of the board if her proposals are to receive timely consensus approval.

It's in the DNA: Because of the makeup of the board, the members have a tendency to micromanage "their" company. They do not view such actions as interference with management's responsibility and authority.

The Short Term: The qualifications required to manage a cooperative are more demanding than those for an equivalent publicly owned company. Being CEO of a cooperative is akin to being a city manager. The CEO has no say in selecting the board members nor in determining how long they serve. The problem is not that they serve too long. About the time the CEO has trained them to be contributing board members, they rotate off the board. Board members often change every few years. This can be seen in some of the interregional cooperative boards. Likewise, the city manager gets the alderpersons who are elected, all with their own agendas for their own constituencies. If the alderperson is not reelected, then the city manager has a new "director." The process of orientation and education must start all over.

Manage the Personality–Not the Person

Care and Feeding: The CEO of a cooperative must have a strong Chief Operations Officer (COO) to run the business. The CEO will be required to devote a significant amount of time to the care and management of the board of directors. Otherwise, the board will dominate the "hired-hand" and run the organization to the detriment of all concerned. Whereas public companies are thrust into crisis transformation by their CEOs, cooperatives get there primarily due to their boards of directors.

Recommendations: Cooperatives should set a maximum board size of nine members, four of whom should be independent outside directors, each with a different proven skill set that supports the CEO and the organization's strategic direction. The "owners" would still have a majority if required, however. The checks and balances this would afford could counteract the built-in conflicts of interest that have been a significant deterrent to the growth of this business sector of the economy.

Closing thought on boards: The Board of Directors can change anyone in the organization, but only the Board of Directors can change itself.

Transformation Participants

Chapter 4

THE CEO

CEO personality = company personality: Companies are thrust into crisis transformation situations because of the individuals who run the companies. The key individual in any corporation has to be the Chief Executive Officer. The CEO establishes the organizational personality and values under which the company operates. To change the values and culture in a corporation the Board of Directors has to change only the CEO. The corporate culture and the value systems of the company will change within a time span directly related to the size of the corporation. That is, in a small company of 100 employees or so, this can be done in a matter of months. In a large corporation with thousands of employees in multiple locations, it can take up to several years for an effective change to be noticeable.

Bad news is buried, good news is rushed to the top: The CEO must be able and willing to listen to the bad news as well as the good news. Reality requires the CEO to understand intellectually and psychologically the propensity of any organization to "deep six" the bad news and rush the good news to the top. Seldom will bad news ever

rise so high. The bad news that does get to that level will be consistent with the CEO's perceived personality. Organizations seek unanimity even at the expense of intellectual integrity and truth.

The CEO of a company listed with the New York Exchange, frequently out of town, instructs his staff not to disturb him with phone calls except in a dire emergency. He describes what he considers a dire emergency as "Only if my wife should die." The staff perceives that any call could jeopardize their jobs. How much bad news do you think this CEO gets? This attitude and the resulting relationship between the CEO and staff can be a corporate killer.

Transformation cannot be initiated if the change maker cannot recognize the need.

Personality, personality, personality: The personality of the CEO is crucial to the long term survival of the corporation. The CEO is the one individual who determines whether the company should operate in constant transformation or crisis transformation mode. If he does the first capably, then the latter will not be required. The leadership of a CEO with a healthy personality creates an environment conducive to constant transformation. The CEO must lead the organization on an endless journey of transition and voyage of discovery.

The CEO's job and personality qualifications: The CEO or general manager is a leader who has knowledge of a wide range of disciplines but is not necessarily a specialist in any particular discipline. Generally, this person will have moved up through an organization by working in several disciplines and departments. He likely worked in a matrix type organization running special projects. Perhaps he has worked as an assistant to a senior executive to gain oversight and perspective of the overall organization and knowledge of the various disciplines within it. Such disciplines might include engineering, maintenance, operations, finance, marketing and sales, strategic planning, and human resources. A person capable of moving through these various disciplines within a corporation must clearly demonstrate reasoning and strong analytical abilities. He will also have good interpersonal skills. Most importantly, he must be able to stand tall and tough when the occasion demands this behavior, sometimes referred to as "walk the talk."

The educational background of the CEO or general manager for any organization ideally should include the liberal arts. He should have been exposed to the humanities before branching off or specializing in one of the technical areas such as law, engineering, or finance. A liberal arts background offers important benefits.

A broad based general education gives dimension to the person's knowledge and ensures an introduction into disciplines that will not be part of professional life. It allows the opportunity to read and learn about Elizabethan drama, early Chinese history, great naval battles of the 19th century, or other wide-ranging interests.

In addition, the study of the liberal arts demands the development of critical thought and analysis. The student comes to understand that no branch of knowledge is isolated. Every branch of knowledge is enriched by the integration of other knowledge. Correlations are made between the past, the present, and the future. Literature does not stand alone but demands the knowledge of the history, social mores, and economic vibrancy of the times. The student learns that every topic leads to a vast and endless set of possibilities. A driving curiosity and hunger for continued learning are essential.

The study of the liberal arts demands that ideas be tested. No new knowledge is accepted without rigorous examination and integration with information from other sources. The result can be a confidence in facing life's complex experiences and, as I was once told, "a comfort in the company of one's own mind."

If the person being developed for the CEO or general manager position has not been exposed to the liberal arts, this should be done early in the development process. This can be accomplished by sending the candidate to an institution that specializes in this area of executive development. The Aspen Institute of Humanistic Studies,* for instance, offers an outstanding ten-day course, The Aspen Institute Executive Seminars. These seminars

---

* The Aspen Institute, 717 Fifth Avenue, New York, NY 10022, 212.759.1053

are designed to provide a significant personal and professional experience for business executives and leaders from varied sectors of society in the U. S. and abroad. Such educational experiences provide an opportunity for executives to come together for reflective examination of the great ideas expressed throughout history and relates them to fundamental issues confronting humanity.

These seminars expose the developing executive or general manager to the writings of the greatest minds from Plato, Aristotle, Socrates, the Bible, Darwin, Nietzsche, Freud, Maslow, Melville, Hobbs, Locke, Rousseau, Machiavelli, John S. Mills, Tocqueville, and Marx to modern day writers as far ranging as Franklin D. Roosevelt, Martin Luther King, Lodge, Schumpeter, Freedman, Bluestone, and Harrison.

These ancient and modern readings are analyzed to relate the writings to current issues and debate how they can be applied in dealing with our interpersonal relationships as well as our social problems. For example, the Chinese philosopher struggling with the issue of whether man is good or bad is discussed in the context of the tragedies occurring in the Balkans and in Africa. The declaration of women's rights delivered in Seneca Falls,

NY, in 1848, expands to struggles with the appropriate definition and dealing with sexual harassment in the office place. Plato's philosopher king might find his counterpart in today's corporation.

Continuous education and intellectual curiosity are important. Managers, leaders, and all other people in industry must have a continuing education experience if we as a nation are to be competitive in the global arena. The general manager, although the leader of the organization, frequently deprives himself of continuing education experiences. While he makes sure other management staff attend development seminars and continuing studies, more than likely he does not go. A general manager should have as part of his job description the requirement to regularly attend appropriate courses in continuing education to recharge his intellectual curiosity. The leader must engage in intellectual aerobics. Ideally, he should go to institutes outside his own field of expertise. One test of potential for management is the willingness to spend some time learning new skills. Look at credentials not only for success in running organizations but also for flexibility in going to school or learning new skills not directly related to specific interests or background.

For example, a general manager of a chemical industry or equally demanding technical industry really should be expected, in our view, to take time to study courses that would broaden his general knowledge in other fields. For example, one year it might be literature, the next year art, music, history, or a foreign language. The sole criteria should be that the subject be outside his technical field. Each course should be in a new area, in which he would have to attain a minimal degree of competence. This would not only stimulate learning ability and adaptability but could also expand what he can provide for the people he serves as supervisor, manager, and leader.

What is in Your Bag of Rocks?: This proposed exercise in learning provides a greater understanding and appreciation of life. It also provides an opportunity for a person to stop and examine his bag of rocks from time to time. We all are brought into this world with a bag of rocks which are a result of history repeating itself in the form of biases, cultures and value systems which derive in descending order from 1) our parents, 2) our peers, 3) our church, and 4) our schools.

Unfortunately, most of us carry this bag of rocks around as we go through life. We never stop to examine what is in the bag. We seldom, if ever, stop to question these "articles of faith." Our parents, teachers, peers, and others implant "truths" in us that reflect their biases and perceived truths. They may be true for us, and they may not be. This proposed training for the general manager and for the developing management of any corporation should provide time to stop, empty out the bag, and go through it rock by rock. Honestly ask yourself, "Do I or do I not still believe this? Does it conform to my value system? Is this still germane to my life, to what I am doing, to what I plan to do?"

If with an open mind we are true to ourselves, we will from time to time add another stone because of the intellectual insight as a result of the continuing education courses and training sessions. More than likely the number of stones discarded will exceed the number added. We believe that it is essential that we stop and look into our own souls. We need to contemplate our origins, destinies, and aspirations. If you would continue to serve people as manager and do it humanistically, look quietly inward. Know thyself.

Specific features of the successful CEO: The choice of a CEO can be made on a political basis, a previous track record at other companies, or by careful assessment.

Manage the Personality–Not the Person

Elsewhere, Rousey, Morrison, and Deacon (see Suggested Readings, Chapter 1) have published research showing some rather specific features of a person who would be successful as a CEO. These include good reality testing, a capability for interpersonal relationships, and an absence of any cognitive compromise either by virtue of illness or age, the absence of characterological problems, and the absence of a significant depression. These features can be detected by testing after the selection committee has found candidates suitable to them on both a business and an experiential basis.

Recognizing deteriorating leadership in the CEO: The interplay between transformation situations and changing company fortunes can be myriad. Most chief executives like to place blame on issues such as market changes, economics, or foreign competition rather than on their own performance. It has been the authors' experience and remains their belief that companies permit themselves to descend to the unfortunate position of requiring crisis transformation of their operations solely because of the quality of leadership or the lack thereof. This can be caused in large part because the entity has a CEO who requires a great deal of both cognitive and emotional structure. In our experience, this is a significant personality weakness for a

CEO. It is neither conducive to nor compatible with leadership.

The need for crisis transformation can also occur because of a failure to recognize deterioration in the leader's mental capabilities. For instance, there are cases of rather significant misdirection of strategy by companies at the behest of the CEO when it was later found that the CEO was suffering from mental decline. For instance, the onset of brain tumors, dementia, and alcohol/substance abuse are not always obvious. This can certainly cause a very subtle and insidious type of reduction in capability. It isn't always obvious to that individual or to the supporting staff. Even if it becomes recognizable by the staff, seldom does one dare lay his career on the line by making such a suggestion. The downside is that failure to do so may well lead to the demise of the company as well as the carefully guarded career.

Unfortunately, cognitive and emotional impairment sometimes occurs secondary to surgery. Unless you resort to acupuncture, major surgery usually requires the use of very potent anesthetics. The object of the anesthetist is to administer only that necessary for the level of surgery. However, major surgery requires that the patient be anesthetized to a very deep level with the intent of rendering the physiology of the person as close to death as possible without losing him over the edge. Major surgery can require the application of potent chemicals for as long as several hours. In some instances following major surgery, we have seen scrambled thought processes for several months. This may be manifested by difficulty in expressing complete sentences. Fortunately, this is usually a short-term side effect as the body does dissipate these chemicals over time. However, management should be aware of this potential temporary disability and review thoroughly every decision of a manager for the first six months after major surgery.

Protecting the CEO: One of the ways an organization can protect against a dysfunctional state in a CEO is to require both an annual physical examination and annual psychiatric examination. The law requires privacy in both of these areas. One way the physical examination can be dealt with while fulfilling the legal aspects is to require the annual physical examination as a condition of continued employment. If the employee submits the results to the Human Resource Department, then the company will pay for the physical examination. If the employee chooses not to submit the results or have the doctor submit the results to the Human Resource Department, then the employee is required to pay for the physical examination. Typically, a psychiatric examination is done on the basis that the employee can determine what, if any, portion is to be revealed to the corporation and to whom in the corporation. A psychiatric examination can provide management an early warning system to indicate whether further examination or treatment should be undertaken at an early date to prevent potentially large and costly misdirection of the corporation. It is commonplace for corporations to provide Employee Assistance Programs (EAP). Such help should be available to all levels of management, including the CEO. A healthy CEO is vital to the corporation.

Transformation Participants

Chapter 5

TRANSFORMATION MANAGERS

THE CRISIS MANAGER: A SPECIAL PERSONALITY

A crisis transformation situation demands a crisis manager. The crisis manager can be very valuable to a corporation. Most corporations do encounter crises from time to time. The great crisis manager comes in one model only—super-hyper-speed. He is a highly charged individual who relishes a difficult situation. He sees the difficult situation as a challenge to his capabilities. The more difficult the situation, the higher the flow of adrenaline and the more charged he becomes. No doubt, you have spotted such an individual. Just look for a crisis, and you will find one individual "in charge." A person with this Type A personality cannot tolerate a vacuum in leadership, so he assumes control. He has fifteen balls in the air at any given time and a phone in each ear. He makes on-the-spot decisions and issues orders, which can be translated, "Do it my way, and do it now!"

PERSONALITY TRAITS OF THE CRISIS MANAGER

Decision-making is time-driven: The good crisis manager understands instinctively that all decisions are time driven. He is perfectly willing to make a decision at the moment when it needs to be made, utilizing only the information available to him at that instant. The thought of delaying the decision in the expectation of acquiring additional information never occurs to this personality. He makes the decision and moves right on to the next one. He can throw another ball in the air without ever stopping to second-guess himself. He possesses the self-confidence to know he has made the best decision under the circumstances. Time is the driver.

Superior reality testing is critical: In addition to a genuine Type A personality, a good crisis manager also exhibits superior reality testing. ***Reality testing*** refers to the person's ability to differentiate what is going on in the environment from his own internal feelings about the situation. He doesn't get them mixed up. He knows that if something is going down the drain, it's going down the drain. He doesn't confuse this fact with his feelings about whether it should or shouldn't. He accepts the fact that the situation is deteriorating and deals with it. He is able to extract the significant data for solving the problem from all the extraneous data. Once he has done this, he can ignore any irrelevant data, including his own feelings, which may or may not coincide with the "real" facts.

The crisis manager demands recognition: While the ideal crisis manager is supremely confident, he also requires recognition. "Hey, look at me! Look at what I'm doing. Am I great or what?" You have seen the crisis manager at the scene of a fire or similar disaster, standing in the limelight giving directions right and left. He leaves no doubt who is in charge. Wow! What attention! His need for recognition shows.

***The crisis manager sets things right*:** Another dynamic is his unyielding conscience and a need to set things right, according to his own rigid standards. Without the sense that things are absolutely right or wrong, the crisis manager has no guideline from which to operate. He must be sure of what is right and what is wrong, tempered by the reality of the situation. Then he can resolutely march forward and rectify the situation. In essence, he asserts, "Get out of my way! This is the way it's going to be done, because I know it is right." Usually, due to his superior reality testing, it is right.

From a psychological standpoint, the crisis manager is rushing in to save the organization from going down the tube. To paraphrase the old vaudeville play, the house is

about to be repossessed, and the villain says, "Pay the note, or else!" The role of the crisis transformation manager is that of the hero who rushes in to save the damsel in distress.

Perhaps on an even deeper level, the crisis transformation manager is recreating an earlier experience in his own life. He may be trying to rectify by his own behavior an experience he had in his own family. For instance, if his father had lost the family fortune, he might continually try to redo this earlier trauma by saving the family (or the organization). He acts in a competitive way to show he is stronger than his own father, who couldn't save the family. Thus, the behavior of the crisis transformation manager not only has a positive function for the organization, but it also has some adaptive healing function for the crisis transformation manager himself. The organization that employs a crisis transformation manager has to know the limit beyond which his behavior may become destructive to the organization.

The crisis manager is highly competitive: Another requisite for the crisis transformation manager is that he be highly competitive. He tries to demonstrate to his employer that he is up to solving this crisis and even that he is the best in his field.

The traits are characterological: The personality traits we have identified with the crisis manager are likely characterological. That is, to the crisis manager, his behavior doesn't seem at odds with his view of how life should be. He proceeds in his course of action without any qualms. The executives above him, however, can appreciate that once the crisis is resolved; they should stop acting as if things are still in perpetual crisis.

Crisis management requires intelligence: Another significant psychological characteristic is that the successful crisis manager obviously has to be intellectually well endowed. Without the superior mental capability to acquire a knowledge base and analyze the situation, the other psychological issues are really beside the point.

NECESSARY SKILLS AND KNOWLEDGE

We believe management skills are transferable from industry to industry. The crisis manager must possess the requisite management skills. The most critical requirement of the crisis manager's job is working with and managing personalities.

Also, the crisis manager should have at least a minimal knowledge of the macro characteristics of the industry setting of the organization and of the micro-characteristics (technical skills) peculiar to the industry. For instance, if the individual is working in a chemical plant, he needs to be acquainted with the fundamentals of the chemical industry (macro) and have some knowledge of the technical aspects of this particular operation (micro). This need for particular knowledge would apply to the automobile industry, running a hospital, or making widgets. If this minimal technical knowledge base is present, the overall management skills and management techniques are transferable from one industry to another.

Manage the Personality–Not the Person

We concede that in some fields, such as research and development, technical knowledge could take precedence over people skills. In that case, it would be best to find someone who has both technical and management training and experience. Even in these fields, management requires people skills as well as technical skills, and we are probably talking about degrees rather than magnitudes.

The crisis manager must be able to interpret outside data to drive his strategic plan for the crisis transformation. It is even more important to understand the inside data, the technical and personality capabilities of the inherited staff. For most situations, the requisite technical skills can be taught in a short time. The crisis manager must have the personality characteristics to carry out the required management functions.

The leader's personality sets the pace: If the company requires a crisis transformation, then by all means go find a crisis transformation manager. The organization must operate in a crisis mode. The urgency of the financial situation seldom permits the luxury of the time required for consensus management. The leader has to make drastic decisions quickly and stand up to them. You have good reason not to rely too heavily on the "inherited" people's abilities, at least until results have proven otherwise. They are the same people who operated the company into the need for a crisis transformation. In a turnaround situation, a good crisis transformation manager can make the difference between success and a Chapter 11 filing. The personalities of the people, especially the personality of the leader, make the difference.

The crisis manager has a high-maintenance personality: The crisis manager can be very valuable to a corporation if properly managed. If not, he is a liability. Keep in mind that the crisis manager is difficult to manage. He requires close attention and constant follow up. You will be wise to invest an above average amount of your supervision time in personality maintenance. His personality requires it. Be sure you understand your own personality as well as that of the crisis manager before you initiate this voyage of discovery.

Constantly monitor the personality: Depending upon the situation, the crisis mode can be good, but it also can be terrifying for the company and for the employees. If the company is in a crisis (financial or otherwise), it needs crisis management. In a smooth-running company, a company without crisis, where the object is to manage or fine-tune the last few cents per unit out of the cost of the operation, the crisis manager can be an absolute disaster. Constant monitoring of performance is required to ascertain the optimum time to remove the crisis manager.

Organizational sacrifices have limits: An organization or staff can only tolerate the rigidity and single-mindedness of a crisis manager for a limited time. For example, if you are in the hospital desperately ill, you can tolerate a specific regime about medication or exercise. Once you get to feeling better, you no longer see the need for the same intensity or single-mindedness. At that point, you are likely to either get mad at the doctor who is giving it to you or follow it less rigidly. In an organization, people may sabotage the organization as a silent protest.

Do not leave the crisis manager in the management slot too long: How long is too long? He should be removed as soon as the situation returns to "normal." Otherwise, the crisis manager will find the "normal" operation boring. It will neither challenge him nor provide him adequate recognition. He will require the creation of a new crisis to manage. If you see this happening, then you have left the crisis manager in position too long. Senior management must constantly monitor the crisis transformation manager and remove him at the appropriate time. This can be done humanistically. When you move him out, recognize his accomplishments, contributions, and value added to the organization. He may move upstairs to an appropriate position to await the next company crisis.

Utilize the crisis manager only to manage a crisis and only as long as it takes to return the operation to a

reasonable level of normalcy. Then remove the crisis manager and replace him with one who has the personality to operate in a constant transformation mode.

THE CONSTANT TRANSFORMATION MANAGER

The management style for constant transformation is significantly different from the crisis transformation mode. Constant transformation requires relationships, credibility, support, trust, and love. The constant transformation manager will encourage their development.

The crisis manager, in contrast, charges in on his white horse with six-shooters strapped to his hips. He is determined to make things happen his way, now. The time to pick up the pieces and patch up relationships comes only after the company has been saved.

Sadly, very few people can make the transition from crisis transformation manager to constant transformation manager, not only because of the different personality requirements, but also because the permanent management team members have too difficult a time trusting someone who has just forced them to make such sacrifices.

The constant transformation manager (or project manager) requires many of the same personality features as the crisis manager. Both managers should be determined, independent, decisive, productive, courageous, and visionary. Both have good reality testing and are extremely confident.

Primary personality differences between the crisis manager and the project manager can be found in their temperaments. The crisis manager operates closer to the edge of chaos than the project manager, who strives to keep his operation running smoothly. The crisis manager requires recognition by others, while the project manager is content to do his job without fanfare. The job itself satisfies his need for validation. The crisis manager is often more outgoing, charismatic, responsive, enthusiastic, and care-free. The project manager is a gifted, analytic, conscientious, and perfectionist individual. These traits help him carry out the fine-tuning required in a constant transformation.

Constant transformation allows more time for information gathering and decision-making. It also allows for the development of relationships and consensus. People skills continue to be extremely important in constant trans-formation management.

Transformation Participants

Chapter 6

THE SUPERVISOR

The Interface: Other than the CEO or general manager, the most crucial supervisor in any corporation is the frontline supervisor. The frontline or firstline supervisory level is the interface between the exempt and the non-exempt, or between managers/leaders and the technicians. Corporate America has typically chosen the frontline supervisor from the technicians. The term *technicians* includes maintenance, accountants, process operators, etc. Management chooses the best technician and promotes her to be the next supervisor. This is particularly true in non-union shops. A technique commonly used in union shops is for management to pick the most rabid union technician and promote her to first line supervision. This could accomplish the goal of making an immediate conversion from anti-company to pro-company and, at the same time, remove a sticky thorn in the company's side. Neither of these tactics is recommended. The problems created are far greater than those solved.

One positive equals two negatives: Whenever a company takes the best technician and promotes that technician to frontline supervisor, it has accomplished two negative things in one fell swoop. The company has just lost its best technician and likely has created the worst supervisor in the company. The personality requirements to be a top technician are not the same as those required to be a first-rate supervisor. Ideally, the technician requires a highly structured environment because the technician is required to perform the same activities in the same way again and again. By design, the chores of the technician require a repetitive discipline of always performing them in exactly the same fashion without experimentation and without personal adventure. This is the essence of ISO-9000. Doing otherwise can lead to less than the desired result. There is little or no ambiguity in the work of the technicians because it is highly structured and repetitive.

Ambiguities do not phone ahead: On the other hand, the supervisor position, by its nature, is neither repetitive nor highly structured. The supervisor has to deal with people who by their personalities are all different. They come one of a kind. The supervisor must be able to deal in ambiguities. The leadership requirements of the supervisor are ambiguous. The requirements for the technician are more structure and less ambiguity with this ratio shifting to more ambiguity and less structure as she assumes a supervisory role. The imposition of ambiguity will frequently arrive in the form of a minor to major crisis. The supervisor is required to immediately assess the problem to determine the magnitude of the crisis and to prioritize it into the structured plans that she must constantly monitor, supervise, and change.

This was seen in a case where the maintenance department had scheduled all of the available person-hours for the day via the Maintenance Planning and Work Control program. Suddenly the maintenance supervisor received an emergency call that three chemical railroad cars had been derailed inside the plant. This required an immediate rearrangement of the maintenance personnel from a planned environment to a reactive environment because the cars must be taken care of immediately to assure that this potential safety hazard will not cause further danger. Secondarily, it is important not to delay other shipments from the plant. This requires a complete rescheduling of the maintenance technicians and a complete rescheduling of the use of the heavy equipment from other jobs in order to correct this most critical situation. This is followed by a rescheduling of the planned jobs in terms of required completion based upon safety, health, and plant operations priorities. For the more urgent work orders, this could require working overtime to complete them and bring them back within the overall schedule.

The proper handling of this type of emergency cannot be scheduled. If it could be scheduled, then it would not be an emergency. This is ambiguity. The situation demands turning the finely tuned plans for the day upside down. This is change. This causes stress. This requires a special personality profile to handle these types of situations effectively and efficiently.

Sometimes people handle stress by developing physical aches and pains or by resorting to alcohol or substance abuse. Management needs to know if an individual is prone to such a coping style. If so, then management needs to monitor the individual and provide her with an opportunity to express stress in other more appropriate ways, place her in a new position, or terminate her. The development of stress related symptoms could be costly to an organization. This cost may manifest itself as medical leave, absence from work, or decreased functioning while at work. There may even be some spillover to an individual's personal and home life. This infiltration of the employee's personal life may take its toll in terms of her marriage or the health and well being of members of her family. An employee at any level–from the CEO to the lowest skilled and compensated individual–who has problems outside of work brings them to work. Providing employee assistance programs for all levels of employment

is a wise investment in the organization's success.

Choose the personality first: The next frontline supervisor should not necessarily be chosen from the ranks of the technicians because few companies can afford to lose their best technician. Neither can they afford to have an inadequate supervisor. It is suggested that a separate development track be established to create a potential pool of supervisors based upon personality characteristics. In an operating plant, this is best done by hiring young engineers with appropriate personality characteristics, training them in the fundamentals of the operation, providing them with supervisory training courses, and exposing them to concentrated education in the liberal arts, particularly in the area of psychology. Then, gradually increase their areas of responsibility until they are ready to be moved into the supervisory role.

The selection of the candidates for this position is a most critical issue as engineers and accountants are typically trained as technicians. Within these ranks, it is important to choose, by interview and testing, personalities that have the flexibility and the ability to deal with ambiguity. Because interviews arc so dependent upon the interviewing skills of the person conducting the interview, they are not consistent in predicting, with any high degree of accuracy, the future success of the person.

Personality first, then training: Placing the individual in charge of a specific project can enhance the preparation for the supervisory role. Shutdowns for repairs provide an opportunity for such projects. This provides supervisory experience on a very limited scale but also permits a real life look at how the trainee communicates plans, executes, and interacts with the technicians. Depending upon progress made through such tasks, the assignments can become more frequent and of increasing responsibility. This progressive approach also acquaints the future supervisor with the technicians and more importantly acquaints the technicians with their future leaders.

The Liza Doolittle refrain: "Why can't a woman be like a man?": This refrain is heard repeatedly in the show *My Fair Lady*, about the remaking of Liza Doolittle. This same refrain is heard in the management ranks in nearly all organizations, with a slight variation that goes why can't so and so be like Joe, or why can't she be like Amy. The answer to this is very simple and straightforward: no one else is like Joe and no one else is like Amy. Everyone is different. Therefore, everyone brings a different personality to work. Up front, the effective supervisor recognizes that she is not dealing with one agglomerated personality but is managing a number of individuals, each with very distinct and unique personalities, each with different maintenance requirements. These differences require different considerations in each case. For this reason, no two people can be managed effectively in exactly the same way.

Another reason that argues well for personality testing is that if you have a clear read on both the personality to be managed and the personality doing the managing, then you have overcome a major impediment to effectively interfacing with that individual's personality. Very often, ineffective supervision is caused by the personality of the supervisor rather than that of the person being supervised. We make this statement primarily because of the less than scientific approach companies have typically employed to select supervisors. Recognize the uniqueness of the personality; capitalize on the strengths, and manage the weaknesses. Manage the personality, not the person.

Transformation Participants

Chapter 7

SELF-DIRECTED WORK TEAMS

Many companies have addressed the frontline supervisor issue by eliminating this position altogether. The result is the ***Self-Directed Work Team (SDWT)***. Collectively, it directs its own activities to achieve the company's goals without immediate supervision. This effort has met with great success when the preparation has been adequate and the work environment chosen with care. All persons in the SDWT must be highly trained, be certified to perform in all positions of the unit, and have empowered themselves.

Empowerment: Management must provide the environment to make empowerment possible for individuals to fulfill these expanded responsibilities. Empowerment is not ladled out by management. It is assumed by the empowered. Management must permit the assumption of empowerment. This cooperative work effort by empowered, well-trained people has been very successful for the companies that have been brave enough to venture forth and break the age-old mold that requires someone to continually watch over the technicians. The SDWT has been utilized extensively in highly automated minimally

manned operations, such as those in the chemical industry. Such operations provide a natural environment for this type of management.

Balance the SDWT personality profile: We believe it is important to balance the personnel personality profile of SDWTs to maximize the cooperative interaction required for success. Utilization of the SDWT can address the challenges inherent in developing the first line of supervision. Although the SDWT is not without challenges, it does offer the advantages of permitting empowerment, increasing self-esteem, promoting and demanding teamwork, placing responsibility at the lowest practical level within the organization, and optimizing costs incurred in any production effort.

The old culture dies very slowly: Why aren't more companies using this exciting and economical approach to operations? There are lots of excuses, not many reasons. The primary excuse is apathy. It is easier to maintain the status quo of top-down management (at least until the crisis catches up with the status quo). Significant change in the corporate culture entails work and stress to be managed.

SDWT requires change in the corporate culture: Do not underestimate the difficulty of the change required. You must move from a culture in which the individual is directed and does only what is required to one in which the individual is asked to commit to participate in defining and performing the job effectively and efficiently. Senior managers and CEOs say they want empowered SDWTs, but they feel compelled to maintain some top-down controlled programs. This conflict can confuse and confound the troops, undermining the commitment necessary for successful SDWT. To eliminate this perceived confusion in direction, management must recognize and communicate the conflicts, air the complaints, and clearly define the parameters of decision making permissible to the members of the SDWT. This appears to offer the best chance of making these conflicting directions understood and workable.

Implementing the SDWT is difficult: Even with these best efforts, the facility environment may not be conducive to this type of endeavor. The personnel may not possess the required personalities to be successful. Although this may look easy on paper, the implementation is very difficult because of the built-in conflicting directions and the significant changes required in the corporate culture. In spite of these many problems, we can expect to see the SDWT used more and more in our drive for world-class competitiveness. The high priced babysitters (frontline supervisors) will have to go.

Personality problems affect the SDWT.

We have discussed psychological and personality factors which contribute positively or impair functioning in the CEO, manager, and supervisor. For these roles, management has only one primary personality to consider. In the SDWT, there are obviously many more persons and personalities involved. It will be helpful to consider some of the possible personality complications that can occur in individual members of the SDWT. Also, refer to our later discussion of personality problems. Personality problems need to be managed. If this is not possible, transfer the individual to another area or put him under the supervision of a person who can manage the personality.

Some people subtly cause problems: These people do not openly express their thoughts and feelings. Instead, they express anger or disagreement in devious ways. This can be devastating in the work environment. One particularly troublesome approach is to get fellow workers to engage in behavior that makes people angry or otherwise sabotages production. These persons are not easily identified. Such individuals appear innocent of causing any

disruptive behavior. Their feelings are not readily apparent to their peers or their supervisors. Unless recognized, this behavior is almost like "the perfect crime." This personality can and will kill off an otherwise successful SDWT.

In any given incident, look for the person you instinctively feel is the least likely to cause trouble. Obviously, you have to be careful not to misidentify a solid contributor. Note the composition of any group in which problems arise. Usually, one person will be present at the point of discord consistently over time. Once identified, he should be given two equally acceptable choices about his place in the SDWT. Both choices should lead to the ultimate goal of management. For example, if the goal is increased production, give the person a choice of two methods, either of which would increase production. If this maneuver does not lead to increased production, he should be transferred to another area where he is less likely to cause a problem or be terminated. Failure to address this personality's disruptive behavior is destructive to the person as well as to his fellow workers and to the organization.

Immaturity and self-importance can disrupt the SDWT: Some people are so childish that they cannot share the workload. Others are so enamored of their importance that they cannot bring themselves to cooperate unless they are the center of attention. Recognizing such personalities is an important step for management. Whether it can be tolerated depends on how much it affects productivity and morale in other workers. Confronting such individuals is usually not fruitful since these personality traits are often quite fixed and of long duration.

Some people never pay attention to instructions: This aspect of personality will interfere with a SDWT. If there is a medical problem such as hearing loss or some emerging problem secondary to disease, management should make a referral for treatment. Even severe impairment of hearing does not in and of itself prevent a person from understanding directions given visually. Not hearing which is not the result of medical problems causes real difficulties for a SDWT. You can manage this personality. Repeat what you say at least two times. Write down instructions. Require the person to repeat your instructions back to you. If you do this for thirty days, the odds of success are very high. The person will develop the habit of concentrating and will automatically repeat your instructions before you ask. As a rule of thumb, it takes thirty days to make a habit and thirty days to break a habit.

Lack of cognitive skills may impair the function of the SDWT: Some member may have specific deficits or impairments in reading, arithmetic, or other cognitive processes that limit his contribution to the team effort. Establish what cognitive skills are necessary to perform the job, and examine them before employment. If a deficit becomes apparent after employment, it may be addressed through the employee assistance program (EAP) or additional training. If not, it may necessitate a transfer to a job that does not require that particular cognitive skill.

Risky behavior endangers the safety of others: Sometimes, a person frequently “goofs up” and makes minor mistakes. If the person engages in substance abuse, his behavior may endanger himself and others in his work environment. A person who has been in a car wreck or had other head trauma may also exhibit this kind of inappropriate behavior. Due to the reporting constraints imposed on past employers, it is hard to identify a person who has left other jobs because of this behavior.

Persons with marital or financial problems: Worry of any kind comes to work, although it may not be apparent to everyone. An organization’s EAP, known and easily accessible to the employees, can mitigate some of the stress caused by such problems and avoid negative consequences for the SDWT.

Can the SDWT ever work? Given the potential personality problems we have discussed, it is a fair question.

Manage the Personality-Not the Person

We know from experience that work units with the least amount of personality problems are the most productive. The task of management is to recognize and group individuals with as few personality problems as possible. Once this is done, then the person to whom the SDWT reports must understand and manage the personalities in the group. The SDWT can produce exciting results as well as a satisfying work experience.

Transformation Participants

Chapter 8

TECHNICIANS

Technicians is a term used to broadly classify those employees who are not in the supervisory ranks. This includes process people, maintenance people, clerks, accountants, financial types, etc. These positions and the work effort required of these people are by necessity repetitive and structured.

Technical capabilities are essential: Focus on the technical capabilities these people need to operate in the areas in which they have responsibility. Many tests on the market can legally ascertain technical capabilities. Also, check records with respect to work competence and training. You may contact The Psychological Corporation in San Antonio, Texas, or National Computer Systems in Minneapolis, Minnesota, for a complete list of formal tests to be used in evaluating potential technicians.

The past work record is history: You seldom learn anything meaningful from a candidate's past work record. A sophisticated interviewer knows that persons who are laid off or leave jobs often do so on an approved pretext (i.e., change of business focus, hard economic times, etc.). When a person leaves a company, his past performance becomes essentially a closed book. The potential liability for discussing or revealing a past employee's work record has become so great that most companies now will tell you only that this person worked from date certain to date certain and nothing more. If you get more than this from the former employer, be assured you are hearing a statement agreed upon by the former employer and the departed employee. The odds are the prepared statement is being read to you verbatim. This is the safe way for the past employer.

This legal necessity adds a degree of difficulty for the potential future employer. Candidates with good work records suffer under this legal restraint, while poor performers live another day to impose their inefficiencies and personality deficiencies upon one more organization.

On the other side of this issue, this potential liability prevents or certainly discourages an individual in a company from carrying out a vendetta against a departing employee by giving bad references. The employee may have been working with a group that was not compatible from a personality profile standpoint. A change to a more compatible environment could improve the person's attitude and commitment, which might positively impact performance.

Gather individual norms on workers who have been successful in each job: Evaluation of the personality is critical. You need to choose the personality that can fit comfortably, or at least with minimum disruption, within the work unit. It is important to know what kind of personality functions well in any given situation or existing work environment. It will help you choose a good personality match for the job.

Develop separate personality profiles for each work unit and organization: This needs to be done periodically. The defined work unit may have changing personality patterns over time due to changes in personnel. Organizations or even subgroups within an organization do not have duplicate personality features. In the same organization, offices on the East Coast and the West Coast will have different personality styles. The failure to fit into an organization to which one has been transferred is well known. Transfer of a worker from a position in Illinois to a similar position in England may fail solely because the personalities of the two groups are different. For example, one may value the open expression of feelings while the other may feel more comfortable inhibiting them.

Standard personality measures require a good deal of time and cost to administer. That is part of the reason conventional personality tests have developed national norms. For reasons discussed previously, this approach does not necessarily solve the problems. The procedure we have used requires significantly less time. It is described in detail in the Appendix of this book. The procedure is equally useful for all levels of an organization.

Technicians, typically, need structure: Choosing this group of employees carries less risk than, for instance, choosing the next supervisor. In our experience, four out of five people will normally fall into the category of requiring structure and are very comfortable in a structured atmosphere. In fact, the same four out of five are very uncomfortable and inefficient in a work environment that is not structured. So, when in doubt, provide structure, because you really can't lose. In the worst case, on average, you will be wrong only one out of five times. That one person who does not require structure, the one who thrives on ambiguity, may well be the next candidate you consider for an opening in the first line of supervision. When you can bat 0.800 without risk, go for the big-league average.

Transformation Participants

Chapter 9

EMPLOYEES

Employees must be empowered. A transformation is a journey of discovery for all the parties involved. To take each individual employee along, the leader must make it possible for the employees to be empowered. Leaders do not empower employees. They can only provide an environment that makes empowerment possible. The employees must empower themselves.

Goal setting: An important part of the empowerment process is to permit and encourage all employees to commit to goals; goals they set for themselves, their families, and the company. A goal is anything you can be, do, or have. All employees must be given the opportunity to achieve to their limits and to be supported in those efforts from the top down. Can you make them do this? No! The leader can only provide the possibility. The leader must refrain from confusing messages. Top-down directives are contrary to empowerment.

Attitude: Goal-setting translates into attitude, a key issue. Attitude is much more important than aptitude. We agree with the premise that aptitude accounts for 15% and attitude for 85% of any accomplishment. Attitude, like a smile, is contagious. A positive change in attitude can make or break the transformation effort. Remember: It is your attitude, not your aptitude that determines your altitude.

The CEO must walk the talk: If the CEO is not prepared to "walk the talk," then no one else will either. Empowerment is very difficult to attain. It requires a cultural change in the way things are done. Management from the CEO down must give up "power" as usually expressed in the typical top-down directed organization. Change causes stress. When we are under stress, we revert to old familiar ways. This makes it critical for the CEO to tell it like it is, and "walk the talk."

Attitudinal and cultural change must spread throughout the organization: All employees should effect their own personal transformations by setting and achieving individual goals. This is crucial for employee commitment. Most people spend more time planning a two-week vacation than they devote to planning their lives. All employees must be given opportunities to lead in their own particular areas of responsibility. As the Chrysler ads that featured Mr. Iacocca emphasized, "You lead, or you follow, or you get out of the way." You cannot lead without followers. Followers cannot follow without leaders. You cannot manage without leading, and the leader cannot lead without managing.

Define the boundaries of decision-making: Each level of decision-making must be clearly delineated for empowerment to work. All of our previous discussion about the positive and negative features of personality as seen in the corporate board, the supervisor, the CEO, the manager, the SDWT, and the technicians apply to the category of employee. All of these foregoing are in reality employees.

Transformation Participants

Chapter 10

UNIONS

The union personality: The company's relationships with union and nonunion employees impact transformations. In the union shop, management often sees and treats the large mass of employees who belong to the union as one large agglomerated personality. The union representative manifests this agglomerated personality to management. The personality of the union representative exemplifies the union personality. (Interestingly, in much the same way, the personality of the company reflects the personality of the CEO.)

The number of grievances equals toughness with the union: Organizations with collective bargaining units (unions) keep score of the number of grievances the union files against the organization. If the grievances are too few, the organization is too lenient. If too many, then the organization is too tough. The problem with this approach is that toughness is not equal to efficiency or effectiveness. Management treats all grievances as if the same personality made them. The erroneous assumption is that all members of the union are like the representative.

The supervisor in a union shop practices a cook-book style of management. Relationships with a union are much less challenging than with a non-union shop. The supervisor operates by the previously negotiated rules in the labor agreement. This agreement delineates the work rules, what management can do, what the union can do, what individual employees can do, even what the negotiated punishments will be for violating specific rules. The supervisor goes by the book, and everyone else does, too.

Are you thinking of decertifying a union? Consider the consequences carefully. What kind of training and cultural change will management and supervisors need in order to manage effectively without the union? They are used to dealing with one individual who represents many. They will have to learn how to deal with many individuals one-on-one. Each individual has his own personality and needs. All parties, particularly those involved in supervision, must undergo a major cultural change.

Going non-union is not an automatic call: For example, a collective bargaining unit represented one operation of a large company. The situation was deteriorating. The company clearly had to choose whether to decertify the union. After careful analysis, management allowed the union to continue. The supervisory staff had spent their entire careers managing with the union. The economic and psychological costs of retraining them were too high. If you must face this choice, be very careful.

Unionization brings cultural shock: If management permits a collective bargaining unit to organize the workplace, the cultural shock will be just as great. The management group must move from managing each person as an individual to dealing with the employees as a group via the union representative. The change can cause extreme stress at all employee and management levels.

Management contributes to problems with unions: The issue of a union versus non-union shop appears in part because of corporate or management problems. A non-union shop headed by a CEO with low reality testing is a prime target for an organizing effort. This person, because of the low reality testing, will not recognize and fulfill the needs of the individuals and will not react adequately to outside data.

If you are a union organizer picking places to organize, make a careful appraisal of the CEO. Go after those CEOs who seem to have low reality testing. This should guarantee the greatest level of success in the shortest length of time for the least money invested. This advice is important. Weigh the cost of organizing versus the expected dues over a given time. Unionism is a business.

If, on the other hand, the CEO has a high level of reality testing, then the organization is likely addressing the specific needs of the individual employees. It trusts them, treating them with dignity and respect. It offers them a challenge, which provides satisfaction in their efforts for the organization. This CEO is reacting to outside data.

For those CEOs who have a low level of reality testing, their best mode of operation is clearly the union shop. If the operation is not already a union shop, then it is likely to arrive at that point sometime in the near future.

Hostile takeover: The unionization of an organization can be understood in business terms as a hostile takeover. The merger and acquisition community has documented and practiced hostile takeovers with much success, particularly during the decades of the 1980s and 1990s.

I shall have no other entity before me: An employee cannot effectively serve two masters at once. Ideally, he devotes his time and energy to forwarding the goals of the corporation, which should be congruent with those of the employee. In a union shop, the employee's first loyalty is to the union and secondly to the corporation. The adversarial relationship that develops between the management of a union shop and the union itself consumes energy. That energy could be more effective if directed to forwarding the goals of the organization and the employees.

Mutual Interests: In all fairness, the leaders of some unions are beginning to understand that the welfare of those they represent is closely tied to the welfare of the organization. They are attempting to develop working relationships that are more open and honest and less hostile and less confrontational.

Nevertheless, the senior author believes it is highly unlikely that a well run union shop can ever be competitive with a well-run non-union operation. He believes that the most effective and competitive form of operation is the non-union shop operated by a CEO who has a healthy personality profile.

Discontent does not hide its head for long: Discontent grows exponentially whenever emotional needs are not met. This growth starts out with one discontented employee. He gingerly voices his perception. A second employee picks it up and passes it on, usually with some embellishment. Because of this exponential factor, a critical mass can be reached before management is fully aware of the problem, particularly if they have low reality testing.

Low reality testing leads to fused emotions: Low reality testing, in this context, refers to the potential for an individual to fuse his emotions with those of others in his environment. This fusion may occur under conditions of group anger, group desire to obtain more freedom in creativity, or group will to present a united front to management. At these points, the critical mass is reached. It becomes harder for the group to back down in any negotiation with management. A similar phenomenon can occur on corporate boards or with management teams designated as negotiators.

The management ranks must be aware of this human phenomenon and always be willing to listen. A great antidote for inaccurate perceptions is an open style of management. Everyone is constantly informed about what is really going on in the organization. If the employees are not told the facts, they will rely on their own perceptions of what is happening. They may invent "facts." There are no secrets in an organization, so tell it like it is. You will avoid damaging morale. People can deal with a lot of adverse news if they believe they are being told the truth. Implicit in a good psychological contract between management and employees is the covenant of truthfulness. Never violate this sacred covenant.

Transformation Issues

Chapter 11

PROACTIVE *VS.* REACTIVE MANAGERS

Proactive management: A proactive manager sets her own agenda and works from it. She controls the situation. The most effective manager is proactive. The ability to set one's own agenda provides the most effective time management available. We as individuals are unequal in many areas. However, there is the one area in which we are all equal. We each have twenty-four hours of time in each day–no more, no less. Time is the great equalizer. The main difference between the effective manager, who moves ahead, and the ineffective manager, who does not, is how well she manages the twenty-four hours in each day. It is essential to be proactive. You cannot effectively manage your time unless you control your own agenda.

Reactive management: A reactive manager works from someone else's agenda and is not in control. The reactive manager is always responding to outside stimuli, always putting out fires. The reactive manager tends to confuse activity with productivity. She does not control her own schedule. If you are not in control of your schedule, how can you effectively manage your time? The answer is you can't. You are a poor manager of your time.

Consider the case of a proactive manager at a low level who always established her schedule two weeks ahead and published it as a rolling two-week schedule. Wide

circulation assured that everyone would be aware of what she had scheduled. The CEO suggested a meeting that would include this individual on a certain date. When the administrative assistant (AA) checked with this individual, she referred the AA to her schedule and said she was already booked on that date. The CEO and three other executives changed their schedules in order to meet her previously arranged schedule. This well organized junior employee rearranged the schedules of four executives.

This is the advantage of being a proactive manager. You set the schedule. You manage your time instead of permitting someone else to do it for you. When chains are jerked, and they will be, be sure you are the "jerker" and not the "jerkee."

If you believe you have the power, you have the power: Power in an organization comes in many guises. It can be manifested by the title, the size of the office, and other subtle ways. However, if you take a proactive stance in the accomplishment of your job, you can assume power far greater than your position or title would indicate. This will not go unnoticed in any organization.

Transformation Issues

Chapter 12

MIS OR MESS

An inadequate management information system {MIS) is a common problem. Organizations that are candidates for Chapter 11 or crisis transformation have one overriding deficiency in common. Three situations may occur. (a) The MIS does not even exist. (b) It is antiquated or certainly not state of the art hardware and software. (c) The MIS is a patch-quilt system with different platforms and software that are unable to communicate with each other.

In one crisis transformation situation, we were surprised to find that the MIS consisted of three computer software systems, none of which could communicate with any of the others. Further, two of the software packages had the distinction of being one of only two such systems in the world and were supported by only one person, the original programmer/system designer of the software. One system supported the financial function and the other supported the Customer Service function. Both functions were critically important to the company. If you were the least bit inclined toward ulcers, this sort of system could be deemed a carrier.

Manage the Personality-Not the Person

The primary requisite for good management decisions is solid information based on reliable data. This is an absolute must. There must be no compromise. To be usable, the information must be current. Providing current data requires a state-of-the-art MIS. Green eyeshades and quill pens just will not get the job done. The computer industry

has advanced to the point where a company can install a network of PCs at a relatively low cost. Off-the-shelf software is available to do just about any job that management may need to provide reliable information for decision-making. Give your company this advantage.

When you walk into a transformation situation, do not expect to find a state-of-the-art MIS. You won't. The previous management has been making decisions using less than timely reliable information or no information at all. Without current reliable information, the organization cannot practice constant transformation and becomes a candidate for a crisis transformation.

THE NINTENDO INFLUENCE

Failed or failing companies are reluctant to move into the twenty-first century in data management. We can only speculate that there is some connection to the age, background, culture, and personality of the senior management. Older CEOs grew up without Nintendo games and computers. Most have a natural aversion to computers. As bosses, they did not directly use them. IBM took full advantage of this knowledge gap for twenty years by installing central processing units (CPUs) with large MIS departments who wrote the programs. They not only controlled the information you got, but also its form. Generally, the programmers gave you what they had readily available. The only options were to take what they offered or wait weeks for the sacrosanct programmers to do their thing. Management dared not question this mystical kingdom.

The older managers retired, and the Nintendo kids grew up and moved into top management. Coincidentally, cheap powerful PCs proliferated. Many companies replaced the CPU with PC networks. Now ordinary human beings can design the forms and extract information for decision-making without relying on the untouchable programmers to provide what the programmers thought was appropriate when they thought appropriate.

Middle Managers–0: PCs–2: The PC on every desk is believed largely responsible for the great exodus of middle management from corporate America. For many years, middle managers served a useful purpose. They were translators of the corporate lingo. They collected the information from the bottom of the organization, massaged it, and translated it into the *lingua franca* best understood by senior management. They performed the reverse function with the edicts and information from top-down management for the workers.

Now that the former Nintendo kids occupy the corner offices, they are perfectly content and comfortable with PCs on their desks. They can operate with the same information the workers generate. They act on this reliable information without benefit of interpretation or translation by middle management. Someone figured out that this expensive layer of "corporate-speak" translators was no longer required. Consequently, the outplacement organizations have been inundated with ex-corporate middle managers.

The technical revolution is finally beginning to pay off for corporate America. It took a long time to get the computer illiterates out of the corner offices. Perhaps this trend will minimize the number of companies trying to operate without adequate and reliable information input to the decision process. If so, this alone should reduce the number of companies requiring restructuring and refinancing, or transforming.

Specific steps: Should a new MIS be required, the following protocol could be considered:

1. Install new or upgrade the present computer system to state of the art. For small to medium sized companies this can be accomplished

economically by using a PC network. NT network software is commonly accepted state of the art for operating the networks. There are others you may consider.

2. Install a first class hard-wire network. Do not scrimp here. This is fundamental to your on-line operating factor for the network.

3. Install off-the-shelf software suited to your management and operating needs.

4. Train someone in the organization in the rudiments of the software packages and network operations so this person can bring the system back up after the inevitable but infrequent crash. This may be a part-time "on-call" task in addition to the person's regular duties. Usually it can be taken care of by training and paying the person, say, an extra $100.00 a month for this added specialty skill and responsibility.

5. Impose the discipline upon the organization to use the system to the maximum as the use alone provides needed structure for the organization.

6. Document the system.

7. Document all changes before they are implemented.

8. Form an MIS committee of users to manage and provide feedback on the performance of the system and needs of the users. This committee can and should be utilized to develop and screen the MIS capital budget.

9. Provide adequate system security.

It is critical to build and maintain an efficient management information system to provide reliable and timely data for decision-making.

Transformation Issues

Chapter 13

STRATEGIC PLANNING

A strategic plan provides guidance for both constant and crisis transformation. It addresses both personality needs for structure and the philosophy on which strategic planning rests.

If a company is in trouble, it probably does not have a viable strategic plan. Management may not recognize the need for a strategic plan, understand how to develop one, or even know one if they see it. If a plan is in place, it may focus more on the final destination or on procedure rather than direction.

A strategic plan is not a destination. It is a journey. This journey must be examined frequently in light of the constantly changing business environment indicated by the outside data. Management should not develop a strategic plan for the company with the idea of using it as a "bible" for the next 3, 5, or 10 years. "Bibles" are forever, directed toward a specific destination. Journeys change constantly either because of outside data or from inside-generated constant transformation.

Participants: Those who will provide the tactical input, impetus, and support to carry the strategic plan to its fruition should develop the plan themselves. The CEO cannot and should not divine the plan, even if she believes she possesses superior and supernatural powers. If top management develops the plan, then the predictable reaction of the "troops" will be "Well, I sure hope old Ms. Ego can make her plan work." The board's predictable reaction will be luke-warm to no support of the CEO's plan. For full support, the Board should be actively involved in the process of developing the plan. The knowledgeable CEO who has a healthy personality and emotional state will solicit input from the outside directors at all stages of its development, while managing the individual personalities of the directors.

Make the plan work. Those who have to execute the plan tactically must support it. When employees, management, and the board assume ownership of the plan and empower themselves through their involvement, they improve their chances of success.

Implementation: In a crisis transformation situation, the leader must involve all the followers, including the board of directors, as soon as possible in the process of

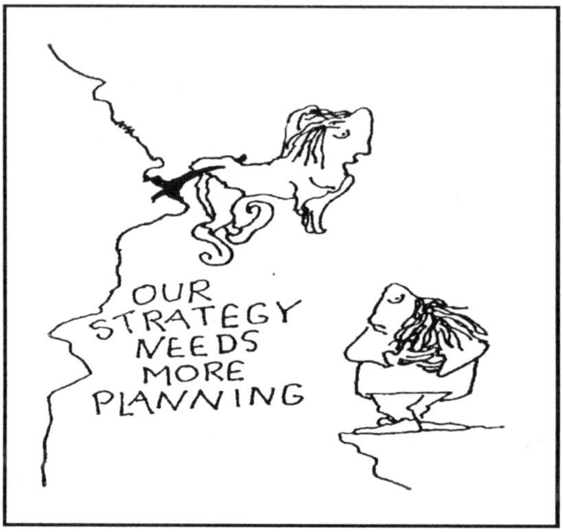

planning the future direction of the company. This is a consensus operation. Consensus frequently takes more time than the leader believes is available or thinks is justified. The challenge for the leader is that she is operating in a crisis mode. The time pressure may tempt her to issue directives top-down instead of relying on those who have empowered themselves to take ownership (commitment) and make the plan work. Deal with this conflict by developing a tight schedule and adhering to the schedule. Do not shortcut this process with the employees or the board. Their commitment to the strategic plan is vital to the success of the transformation.

Discovering personality features: The process of developing the strategic plan is valuable for new management. Evaluating the employees and board members who participate in the process can be very enlightening. Who can think? Who can think strategically? How do they think? How do they prioritize? How do they manage stress? What is their level of reality testing? Are they conservative or venturous, realistic or optimistic? Are they passive or aggressive? Are they deliberate or impulsive? Are they loners or team players? Can they express themselves via the written word? Do they use bullet point general statements that could apply to any company, or do they present clear ideas in essay form, revealing critical thought processes, relationships, and priorities? In addition to providing direction for the company, the planning process provides useful information about the people who will carry out the plan.

The strategic plan drives constant transformation: The strategic plan is the guide for both the crisis and the constant transformation. Once the crisis transformation has been completed, the organization returns to normalcy.

Constant transformation must follow as night must follow day.

Timing: The strategic plan is never done. It must be reviewed frequently to assure that the journey is consistent with the outside data. The plan should be updated and reviewed with the board at least annually. The strategic plan must be revisited regularly and tested for relevance to the outside data. This review permits fine-tuning the organization's performance by constantly raising the bar for everyone–employees, departments, and groups, including the board of directors. This is not only a constant improvement of the same processes or functions; it is an examination of the appropriateness of these processes to meet the entity's changing needs.

Change will be required: That is the nature of a dynamic organization. In the constant transformation, these necessary changes are made incrementally in response to changing outside data. The crisis transformation is time impelled to avoid imminent disaster. It is more jarring. The strategic change of the constant transformation may avert the need for the tactical change of a crisis transformation. The strategic plan provides critical guidance for both types of transformation.

Specific Transformation Problems

Chapter 14

TERMINATION

It is the toughest job: The termination of an employee is the most challenging psychological duty ever imposed upon a manager. The impact of being terminated can be viewed by the employee with a wide range of feelings from total rejection to high elation. When a person has been terminated from an organization, he often has feelings of rejection, unworthiness, and failure. There is a real sense of loss. This sense of loss translates to a loss of identity, a loss of self worth. It can be very acute since most people associate and identify themselves very closely with their jobs, positions, or titles. It is not uncommon to hear a man identify himself upon introduction as Mr. Jones, Manager of Human Resources for ABC Corporation, or other appropriate title. Therefore, the loss of the job equates to a loss of self-esteem and self-worth.

Damaging the family: This loss then immediately expands beyond the individual employee to the family. The financial loss associated with this event can have a very significant impact upon the family. The financial loss can curtail the resources available for entertainment, for schooling, and even basic living requirements.

Diminishing the self: As noted earlier, the loss of a job can also mean the loss of definition of self. Frequently, the male can internalize the loss of a job such that it makes him feel less masculine, less desirable. This is noticeable whether it is the supervisor, technician, or CEO. There is some truth to the slogan, "the title on the door and the

Bigelow on the floor" define the worth of the person. Because of this, many retirements of CEOs are unsuccessful. They really do not understand who they are as people apart from their jobs and consequently do not manage the loss of identity well.

Loss of identity: The impact of the loss of job cuts across all levels from the person who cleans the floors to the CEO. This loss of identity and self worth is most acute in those individuals with low reality testing; that is, those who have trouble separating their feelings and perceptions from the real facts of the situation. This can lead to strange and sometimes almost bizarre actions by the affected person. In the case of a retired senior officer, there may be attempts to prevent the final cutting of the umbilical cord with the faint hope that somehow the company will reconsider all of the past good work and take him back. This type of behavior only delays the healing process. You must make a clean ending before you can make a new beginning. Depending upon the personality and prior planning, this can take from a few months to forever. Early planning is essential for a successful retirement. One reference regarding retirement presented in *Business Week* is on the following Internet sites.

http://wwwbusinessweek.com/1998/29/b3587001.htm

http://wwwbusinessweek.com/1998/29/b35870030.htm

http://wwwbusinessweek.com/1998/29/b3587013.htm

http:wwwbusinessweek.com/1998/29/b3587015.htm
through 3587034.htm

http://wwwbusinessweek.com/1998/29/b3587036.htm
through 3587038.htm.

Manage the Personality–Not the Person

Plan ahead for being unemployed: Whether or not the labor market is unsettled as it was in the late 1980s and early 1990s, all employees should have plans that include what steps to take in case the next round of downsizing catches them. The best planning step to prepare for this eventuality would be to set a budget that consumes no more than 80% of the income stream. This may require sacrifice.

We believe that the sacrifice is well worth the effort. This not only provides a savings nest egg for the "rainy day," but also establishes a standard of living at 80% of the current income level. That means you could take a new job at an income level as much as 20% less than your present job without lowering your standard of living. This is a very important psychological point for the person being terminated. The greatest impact on the psyche comes from having to tell the family that they will have to lower their standard of living because the bread winner can no longer yield an income to support the living standard to which they have become accustomed. Think about how much easier it would be for the terminated employee to tell the family, “Yes, I have been caught in the downsizing at the company. However, we have enough savings to carry us for at least one year. I am sure I can find another job with an income that will not require us to lower our standard of living.” Contrast this with the case where the family lives from paycheck to paycheck, having to decide at the end of each month which payments to delay until next month. No wonder the question most frequently asked of outplacement personnel by the just terminated employee is "What do I tell my family?” So, if you plan for the worst case scenario and can tolerate that, then anything better becomes an opportunity. Plan ahead. You may be next.

The impact on the one who terminates the employee: The termination of an employee by the supervisor is the most difficult job a supervisor will ever have to perform. Frequently, this involves the termination of someone with whom he has worked with for some time or someone he knows very well from shared community activities or personally from shared family and social interaction. The supervisor is frequently aware of the family situation and the potential impact this action will have or can have upon the ex-employee and the family. The good supervisor loves the person and knows the family as well as the details concerning the family. There is definitely a sense of loss by the supervisor as there is or should be a real sense of failure on the part of the entire management.

Termination–the correct process: In all things, there is a right way and a wrong way, and this applies especially

to the termination of an employee. While a company may follow the letter of the law, that does not necessarily guarantee the termination process will be "right." Being legal does not lessen the impact or the necessity for carrying out a termination in the most humanistic way possible. Every company has certain issues that are causes for immediate termination such as the purposeful endangerment of another employee's life, flagrant violation of safety rules, etc. With these exceptions, the act of terminating an employee because of lack of performance should be a well defined process whereby the employee is first counseled about his deficiencies and consequences in written form, which should be acknowledged by the signature of the employee. If the deficiencies are not corrected over a reasonable time, then, after the second counseling, the employee should be given a second notice. Many companies will terminate at this point; however, the "third strike and you are out" is rather common in an effort to be absolutely sure that the person has been treated fairly and humanistically. Economically, the company has invested a significant amount of resources in training this employee and is not anxious to see this investment walk out the gate for other than well founded reasons. Whether it is two or three strikes, do it for the benefit of the company and for the benefit of the employee.

Today, many companies provide outplacement services for terminated employees. Again, there is a right way and a wrong way to provide this service. It is recommended that once it has been determined that an employee is to be terminated and outplacement will be provided, the company should have the outplacement service readily available. The scenario should go something like this: With the outplacement service person immediately available in the next room, the employee is called in, presented the facts in detail (absolutely no arguments), told that he is being terminated, and informed that the company is providing outplacement services. Two corporate management people are present. One talks; the other is a witness. Then, immediately escort the employee to meet the outplacement representative. The safest way to do this step is to read from a script. Keep it short. This minimizes arguments, which can easily yield inadvertent statements that can be damaging. The script provides a necessary record in case of a later lawsuit. This is a very effective and economical way to perform a termination as the provision of outplacement service prevents many, many lawsuits. Never, never get into an argument with a departing employee over any of the issues. Especially avoid discussing the reasons why the employee is about to be an ex-employee. The reasons will have previously been stated in the written notices given the employee or by general decree in the case of a demassing or multiple layoffs or the elimination of positions.

The tendency is to take this last opportunity to let the departing person, who certainly is known and may be a friend, know that you are sorry and really had nothing to do with this, as it was someone else's fault. Don't yield to temptation. This is a tough task to carry out well. Be surgical, do it by the script, get it over with, and have no comment. Let the experienced outplacement person handle

the rage, disappointment, and all the other feelings the person will have. Failure to follow these guidelines may result in arguments that are the bases for frequently successful lawsuits.

What do I tell my spouse? The most difficult question which a terminated employee has to answer is what he will tell the family when they return home. The outplacement people are expert in this area and can develop a statement, which is acceptable to the employee and to the company. This agreed statement (and nothing else) is told to whomever may inquire as the reason for the departure. Departure from this statement can bring lawsuits. Outplacement service is typically provided to the top and middle management. There are also outplacement services available for lower level positions that can assist in writing resumes, coaching for interviews, etc. Companies can and frequently do provide these services in case it becomes necessary to terminate the services of a large number of employees, due to reasons other than cause, such as downsizing, reengineering, or discontinuing a product line, etc.

Termination is a very important undertaking: Treat it as such. The termination of any employee, particularly a long-term employee, is not something to be taken lightly by the organization. It is recommended that no employee be discharged without a prior detailed review of the recommendation and approval by the CEO. This review has been used very successfully in small and medium-sized companies. Even companies with up to $1 billion in sales have used it effectively. The way this works is that the requisite first and second counseling notices and written memos are discussed with the employee. The employee signs the memos, which confirms that he has received and read them and understands the consequences. The recommendation for termination, including reasons, is sent to the CEO. The CEO questions the supervisor making the recommendation and the employee about how and why the company failed and why the employee should be terminated at this time. The employee is free to rebut any comments.

Other beneficial fall out: This procedure has the advantage of smoking out any potential personality bias or differences between the supervisor and the employee. Remember, we have warned you that differences between the supervisor and technician can often reflect a deficiency in the personality of the supervisor as well as the technician. Do not always assume the technician is at fault. The CEO interviews the employee who has been recommended for termination before any final decision is made.

Not only does this review process minimize the effect of bias. It also sends a strong message to all employees that they can expect a fair hearing before any such drastic action is taken. This procedure opens up channels of communication throughout the organization that are normally unavailable to the CEO. It ensures integrity at all levels that might not otherwise be present. It can be a very strong deterrent for the non-exempt people considering a union to represent their interests. The perception of termination without adequate cause is one of the principal issues unions use to organize the workplace.

Termination is a company failure: Anytime an organization has to terminate an employee, management should experience a feeling of loss. Termination is a clear indication that the organization has failed. It has failed to match the personality and the job requirements. It has failed

to prepare the person and to manage the personality appropriately to perform at a competent level in the job or to keep up with the growth of the job. Or, maybe management has failed to manage the entire company, and the termination is part of the salvage effort. The company has failed. Therefore, it has a responsibility to the person its management terminates.

The employee expends a nonrenewable resource: The company experiences the termination of an employee as a failure, not only by the employee, but also by the organization. It has failed to protect its investment in the employee. Many companies believe that when the employee finishes the workday, he is paid, walks out the gate, and it is all even-Steven. No further obligations for or by either party are implied. The author employed another practice, which relies on the belief that the employee is giving the company more than the workday, because in the process of providing this effort, the employee is also expending a non-renewable resource–a portion of their finite working life. For instance, if you begin work at, say, age 25 and you work until you are 65, you have 40 years as a working career, which is a non-renewable asset. If you spend part of those 40 years with a company and then are discharged, the time you spent there is non-renewable and non-recoverable. You are expending this resource, this asset on behalf of and for the benefit of the corporation. Hence, the company has the obligation to make every reasonable effort to match the personality and the skills of the employee to that of a job where the individual can perform in, at least, a competent manner, and remain employed.

Increase the company's investment and the employee's skills: An important part of the psychological contract between company and employee is that the organization has the obligation to constantly increase that person's skills by continuous education and training. This is a quid pro quo for the employee's commitment to expend their non-renewable finite resource–time–for the benefit of the organization. Not only is it good business to provide continuing education and training for the employee, but it is also a moral obligation to constantly upgrade that person's capability. The obligation applies not only to the technical side but also to the personality side, so the person will be better able to deal with the people with whom he works and associates. This also best prepares the individual if a change in employment is required for any reason.

A job is an earned right: The distinction should be made here that this concept is significantly different from the Japanese concept of lifetime employment primarily because of an obligation imposed upon the corporation as a result of the expenditure of this nonrenewable asset of one's working life. However, it still is obligatory for the employee to perform, as a minimum, at the competent level of performance in order to earn the right to continuous employment.

An ever-increasing target: It should be noted that the definition of "competent" performance must constantly increase. A corporation cannot continue into perpetuity unless it constantly improves its effectiveness and efficiency. It must be responsive to outside data via constant transformation. Standing still is not an option for the corporation or for the employees. A static entity is a dying entity. Constant training and upgrading of employees' capabilities are necessary if the entity is to be competitive in the world markets. Therefore, the level of performance

required for "competent" rating must ever move up. This can cause those who were marginally above unsatisfactory to fall into the unsatisfactory ranking in spite of the best efforts of the company on behalf of the person.

"Weeding" is part of the transformation: This state should be viewed realistically. What is occurring is the company's requirements are moving more rapidly than the employee's ability to keep up. This can be healthy for the corporation and should be viewed as a necessary part of a progressive growing entity, one that is practicing constant transformation. If the company is constantly increasing the required level of performance, as it must, then one should expect to see a performance-based turnover or termination of people at the rate of 2-1/2% per year due to their inability to perform in a "competent" manner. If this "weeding out" process is not occurring at the 2 to 2-1/2% year on average, then management and the employees should be concerned. This could well indicate a lack of constant transformation within the entity. This heralds a dying company if constant transformation actions are not initiated in a timely fashion. So, under this concept, one can be terminated for cause as long as it is done under a well documented and fully informed set of procedures, which assures fairness and is humanistic.

Downsizing is a euphemistic term for the termination (firing) of a large number of people, usually in a series of waves. Downsizing is not the universal answer to all troubled companies. One cannot save a company into prosperity. Performance is the better choice. However, there have been many cases where the numbers of employees were excessive and each reduction in force grabbed the headlines and frequently improved the market cap. Nevertheless, downsizing is generally undertaken under the guise of making the entity more competitive by reducing costs. This reason sounds more morally justified. Generally a company goes through at least three downsizings to get it right. The built-in resistance to reducing the kingdoms of people is too great to get it correct the first time or even the second time. Supervisors still think that the number of bodies they supervise determines their power. As we shall discuss later, correct downsizing should take place only once.

Survivors feel the guilt: Who reduces one's power base voluntarily without a fight? Very few. This causes the required downsizing to drag out indeterminately. Consequently, we find all sorts of problems for the remaining workers as they try to deal with loss and psychological loss damage control. The loss associated with those who have to leave has been discussed previously. Those who remain often develop what is known as the survivor syndrome. The guilt they feel negatively affects the productivity and efficiency of the organization. The longer the process is dragged out the longer and deeper this decline in productivity continues. Once it is obvious that a downsizing is required, it should be done the right way. From our point of view, the right way is to do it one time and one time only. Tell everyone "This is it." And mean it. Walk-the-talk. One time should be the limit even at the risk of cutting loose too many people. This will limit the damage control necessary to deal with the loss in morale and attendant loss in productivity. The organization can realign itself, the systems can reform, the internal power structures are redefined, and productivity can begin to climb out of the cellar. And management retains its credibility.

Honest communication: One way to do it the right way is to bring in "experts" to review the corporate structure to determine the numbers and qualifications of people required for the transformed organization. Then engage a first rate outplacement company to assist those who are about to be caught up in the exit net. Then, be honest with all the employees and explain in painful detail why this action is necessary and who, how, why, when and where this will all take place. Constantly update the information while the process is underway. Communicate, communicate, and communicate with employees. Remember that people can take a lot of bad news if they know the facts and believe the information to be true. Be as generous in the financial assistance as the company can reasonably afford. After all whose fault is it? It is suggested that the company provide feedback to the survivors as to the progress of those who are looking for a job. Be sure to highlight those ex-employees who better their employment situation. This gives comfort to the survivors and shows that the company really does care. Depending upon the extent of the sense of loss, it can be very worthwhile to bring in a corporate psychiatrist who is experienced in dealing with loss in such situations. Companies that want to be great do these unpleasant but necessary things in a humanistic way.

The politically sensitive termination: From time to time, and particularly in the crisis transformation mode, the manager will have to terminate a high profile employee who is a part of the "old guard." If you are faced with this, we suggest two rules. Rule One: No matter how incompetent the performance and/or how recalcitrant to support the "new management," everyone has supporters and followers. If this person is a high profile member of the "old guard," apply Rule Two. Never slay a sacred cow on Main Street. This tends to draw crowds. Crowds can become noisy and difficult to manage. Crowds can reach critical mass. One leads the cow up a back alley before termination. This can be accomplished by removing the high profile operating manager to an apparent equal staff job. Have this person report to the top executive to better manage his activities. "Assistant to" is a good title that can confer position with limited and controllable authority. It also gives the impression that the "old guard" supports the draconian actions that the new management will have to take in their effort to save the entity. Gradually reduce the influence of the "sacred cow" to that judicious level deemed safe to terminate. When people are making sacrifices themselves, they tend to forget about others.

The "back alley" approaches, although a bit laborious, save time in the long run and speed the transformation process by minimizing the resistance to change. Is it humanistic? We believe it is. It is the best for the most.

Specific Transformation Problems

Chapter 15

PRODUCTIVITY

THE 80/20 RULE AND THE 80/18/02 RULE

The 80/20 Rule is a well-known rule of business. For instance, 80% of a company's business is typically done with 20% of their customers. Eighty percent of accidents are caused by 20% of the people. If you were head of a sales group, how would you allocate the sales effort? Too frequently, the time is spent in roughly the same percentage as volume of products purchased. Only 20% of the sales representatives' time are spent on the hard-to-sell customers, who present the greatest potential for new or increased sales. Instead sales people typically spend 80% of their time on 20% of the customer base.

Where to concentrate your effort: Not all of the people calling on customers or potential customers grasp this logic. They tend to call on those people whom they most enjoy-those who are buying. They tend to avoid the tough customers as much as possible. After all, who really likes rejection? Nevertheless, this tells you where to concentrate the sales effort.

No one lives for rejection, but some personalities handle rejection better than others do. The personality of the successful salesperson does not understand that *no* means ***NO***. It means *no* only to that particular proposal. They modify their sales pitch slightly and try again. The great sales representatives have this ability to handle

repeated rejection with the optimistic belief that the next pitch will get the order–*which it does!* They concentrate on the 20%.

In a plant-working environment, 80% of all the accidents are caused by the same 20% of the employees.

That tells you where you need to concentrate your efforts in order to minimize accidents. The 80/20 Rule is a general guide to directing and setting priorities. Ignore it at your own peril.

The 80/18/02 Rule is a variation of the 80/20 Rule: It includes the very small percentage at the extreme end of the scale. For instance, when your workforce comes in on a given morning, 80% of them really want to do a good job. 18% are ambivalent or satisfied with mediocrity. The last 2% of the people who walk through the doors come in with malice in mind and intent to harm the organization. It is imperative to search out and guard against this 2%. They can do real damage.

Fire the 2%: This 2% may be reacting to some action, real or perceived, that some supervisor has taken, unwittingly or unknowingly. More likely, their reactions are related to destructive personality traits. You should make every effort to screen out these personalities in the hiring process. However, even the best efforts fail and some will get through the screen. It is imperative to guard against this 2% by identifying these individuals and sending them down the street to your competition.

Outside the sigma limits: To discuss the approximately 2% who come in with the potential for disturbing productivity, we need to view where they fit within the Bell distribution curve. Under a normal Bell curve, assuming you have established the right standard of performance, the plus and minus one sigma limits define the "competent" performance population. The +1 sigma to +2 sigma defines above average performance, while the -1 sigma to -2 sigma limits define the persons who are below average and need improvement in their performance. The +2 to +3 sigma defines superior performance while the –2 to -3 sigma defines unsatisfactory performance. The +3 sigma and greater identifies exceptional performers. The -3 and lesser identifies persons who hopefully were not hired. The majority of employees fall into the +1 to -1 sigma population, or roughly about two-thirds will perform in a competent or average manner. Add one more sigma limit on each side and you define the populations who will perform above and below the competent, or average, level. Approximately 13% will be above average; approximately 13% will need improvement. At and beyond the two-sigma limits you will have about 2% who will be superior performers and about 2% who shouldn't have been hired or if they were, be fired. Thus, the constraints of the Bell distribution curve serve as the basis for asserting that approximately 2 percent of the employees coming in to work have a potential for doing the company harm.

The importance of attitude: The supervisor and management should understand that 18% of the workforce can go either way, good or bad, depending to a large extent on the actions of supervisors. One in five needs extra attention and additional direction. You need to convince the 18% that it is in their best interest as well as the company's to do a terrific job. Deal with this 18% of ambivalence by engaging in a program that will create a change in attitude. Move from boredom to excitement.

Attitude is contagious: We have stated previously, that attitude is the main requirement for doing a competent job. If you change the attitude of the 18%, you will also enhance the productivity of the 80% who came in with a good attitude in the first place. Remember, attitude, like a smile, is contagious. Thus, you maximize the benefit to the organization as well as to the employees.

Not on my picnic: When people get up in the morning, many decide either consciously or subconsciously that they are going to have a bad day. That choice belongs to the individual. Whether to have a good or bad day is strictly up to you. No one else makes this decision. If you decide that no one is going to rain on your picnic that day, come hell or high water, it will be impossible to rain on your picnic

Grab the 18%: The ambivalent 18% haven't made up their minds to have a good day or a bad day. So, you have to grab them when they walk in the door. Attitude is crucial to help this group decide first thing that they intend to have a good day. If they have a good day, they will do a better job.

Get more life out of living and more living out of life: Whether we ever admit it or not, most people know when they are doing a competent job and they know when they are doing less than a competent job. Certainly, their peers know who are the outstanding performers and they know who are the incompetent performers. One of the outstanding motivational trainers and developers in the area of changing attitude, making people believe that they can get more life out of living and more living out of life is Ed Foreman and Earlene Vining of Executive Development Systems (EDS) in Dallas, Texas. EDS offers an excellent seminar, which provides an individual menu as to how one, can have a good day every day if one chooses, or, one can have a bad day every day if one so chooses. It is an outstanding program and it has been used extensively by many corporations such as Citgo, CF Industries, and ASHTA Chemicals. Literally hundreds of other companies have used Ed and Earlene and the staff of EDS to change the attitude of employees and their spouses.

Specific Transformation Problems

Chapter 16

STRESS AND CHANGE

Regressing to the Familiar: Regressing to the familiar is a typical response to executive stress. What do we mean by that? Whenever a person becomes over stressed by a particular set of circumstances they tend to seek refuge in the thing(s) with which they are most familiar or with which they are most comfortable. For example, a CEO who had managed a company into rather serious circumstances became under such stress that he spent a great deal of time figuring out who should have company cars. That alone is not too bad, but he also took the time to carefully choose the specific color of car that each person would be awarded, as well as the options. Meanwhile, the more important strategic items that needed to be addressed were either being left to someone else to make the critical decisions or they were being completely ignored. The manager at all levels should be aware of this psychological characteristic, which affects not only his behavior patterns but also those around him.

Managing Change and Managing Stress: Change has become a norm in modern business and the constant in all well managed organizations. Managing the *constant transformation* situation equates to managing constant change. Change causes stress. To manage stress, a manager first must manage change. The object in managing change in the corporate entity is to make changes that will foster improvement; improvement not only in the existing processes, but changing the processes for better efficiency and effectiveness. A further objective is to increase the pace of change to a level that is just short of chaos. This pace will be dictated to a great degree by the personality of the organization. Managing stress becomes a very important issue when management is affecting change. Change, because it is different, causes stress in the employee body.

Reputable stress reduction programs are available to organizations. One such source is the Mindfulness Based Stress Reduction Program at the University of Massachusetts Memorial Hospital in Worchester, Massachusetts. A manager or CEO can call John Kabot-Zinn, Ph. D. (508-856-5849) or any of his associates to obtain a referral to someone in almost every major city in the United States. A good stress related program is not a one-shot experience. It may be an intensive one-week

program or sessions spread over two or more months. Management should insist that any program they engage have follow-up work built into any offering.

Organizational Stress: Although the change or changes may not impact the immediate structured area in which the employee is functioning, the fact they know that it is going on and they can see it happening within the organization, tends to cause a certain level of anxiety throughout the organization. It matters very little whether or not that the change, which is being made, is good or whether it is bad, or, even indifferent. Nevertheless, the impact still seems to cause an increased level of stress in the individual as well as the organization. Organizational stress must be monitored and managed.

For that reason it is imperative that management make an all out effort to explain all of the reasons for the change. Communicate, communicate, communicate. Management must answer all of the who, why, where, when and how questions before the changes are made. This allows for feedback and comment. The barriers to feedback must be identified and removed. Empowered work teams create an environment, which is conducive to feedback regarding the emotional, or stress condition of the team.

Creating the proper environment conducive to honest feedback requires the management to walk a fine line. Such an environment can be perceived as a democracy with management surrendering it authority. On the other hand, it is important for management to make it very clear that because they are inviting comment doesn't mean they are surrendering their right to make the change. This must be accomplished without shutting off comment or feedback. It is indeed a fine line, because the corporate entity in the final analysis has to be an autocracy, not a democracy. Management has to collect feedback if they are to determine what type of actions will be required to assist the employees and the organization in the management of stress. "Feedback" is the breakfast of champions.

Management Theories and Stress: Since we have postulated that change causes stress, we think it is appropriate that we turn the question around and ask if stress causes change. The immediate response to that is that stress does not necessarily cause change. Are there any management theories that do not cause stress? Let's take a brief look at some of the better known theories.

William Ouchi, professor in the Graduate School of Management at the University of California at Los Angeles in *Theory Z: How American Business Can Meet The Japanese Challenge* describes Type A, Type J and Type Z organizations. Dr. Ouchi suggests the internal organization form is an adaptive response to a particular ecological setting. He suggests "that the Japanese (Type J) form represents an adaptation to conditions of homogeneity, stability and collectivism - a form where individual behaviors mesh intimately together. By comparison, the American (Type A) form represents a national adaptation to conditions of heterogeneity, mobility, and individualism - a form where people link tenuously to one another and rarely achieve intimacy."

Theory Z describes the act of Japanese management, (Theory J) and shows how it can be adapted

to American companies. Many of the American companies who attempted to adopt the Japanese concepts of management have been forced by financial realities to abandon some of the sacred covenants, the prime one being IBM's psychological contract that once employed by IBM you have a job for life.

The Theory X and Theory Y merger concepts were originated by Douglas McGregor who for many years was professor at the Alfred P. Sloan School of Industrial Administration at the Massachusetts Institute of Technology. Professor McGregor concluded that a manager's underlying assumptions about human nature would to a large extent determine this manager's style of management. Theory X managers according to McGregor assume that people are fundamentally lazy, irresponsible and need to be watched constantly. This type of threatening manager carried a big stick and did not hesitate in its application. Needless to say, a high level of stress is inherent with this type of management style. Some of our teachers still manage this way; they carry a big red pencil with which to deal with lazy irresponsible students. The Theory Y manager exhibits a kinder view of mankind by assuming that people are fundamentally hard working, responsible, and need only to be encouraged and supported as needed.

This almost Pollyanna view caused a lot of pain when companies tried to change from Theory X to Theory Y management. There was a failure to recognize the importance of the personality. You cannot make a silken purse from a sow's ear. And you can't make a Theory Y manager from a Theory X manager. Also, a group of employees requiring the structure available under a Theory X manager would be lost and be at loose ends under the unstructured Theory Y manager. We should point out the difference between providing structure and employing the close supervision of a Theory X manager. Close supervision is characterized by riding the back of the employee until they get the job done. It is demotivating and inhibits psychological growth in a restricted environmint. Requiring structure does not mean that the person is lazy or irresponsible. Rather, providing structure allows a worker to know the parameters within which they must function. This knowledge frees them to perform comfortably with a sense of certainty within known parameters.

The Theory Y manager's basic assumptions moves the argument one giant step toward egalitarianism and independence, (or at least more of each), in the work place. Neither industry nor its workers were psychologically ready for Theory Y in 1960. However, the generation of the 60's initiated the societal move toward more egalitarianism and more individual independence to set the stage for the self directed work units.

Theory Y and self directed work units each require a hierarchical mode of control because of the impracticality of integrating every one's individual goals 100% into the overall corporate goals. Structure must be provided for a self-directed work unit. With the required support and without direct supervision, the self-directed work unit can function effectively and efficiently, but not without stress.

To our knowledge there is no one pure single management theory in practice today, which eliminates

stress. The management mode is and should be a mixture that fits the situation. It is of interest that many writers claim corporate failures can be corrected by examining and changing business theories.

In the present contribution, we are proposing another way of correcting and preventing corporate failure and the attendant stress that ensues. We are proposing Theory PH (for personality/humanistic), which emphasizes the criticality of evaluating the personality to fit the job requirement and then utilize the humanistic approach to managing. In its simplest terms...fit the person to the job, develop mutual trust, and practice the Golden Rule.

Specific Transformation Problems

Chapter 17

COMPENSATION

The Collective Bargaining Unit: If you are a member of a collective bargaining unit you don't have to worry about your pay raise. You have someone else negotiating it for you on a collective basis. Your individual talents and values created cannot be recognized by compensation. You are in the pool with the good, the bad and the indifferent, the entire +/-3 sigma range of performers. Or, as the normal distribution curve would define it, you are in with the exceptional, the superior, the competent, the improvement needed and the unacceptable. The settlement will be based on average or competent performance. Why try to do better? Where is the incentive?

Solo Uno: If you are not a member of a collective bargaining unit then you are on your own with respect to compensation vs. performance. You negotiate the starting wage coming in and will have to negotiate each increase there after. How do you do this? Do you ask for a raise when you think it is appropriate? Do you ask for a raise on your anniversary of employment? Does the organization have policies and practices that detail compensation issues such as when increases are considered? Good organizations will. If your employer does have such policies and practices does this mean that you never ask for a raise? No. Asking for a raise requires thought and preparation. Keep in mind your raises are controlled for the most part by your immediate supervisor. While this person may not have the total authority to grant or deny; she does have the responsibility to recommend, which is critical to you.

Thought and Preparation: First: get the recommendation for an increase, nothing happens without it. So, planning is required to determine just how you justify this request to your supervisor. You must be completely familiar with the company's procedures with respect to salary handling. This is no secret. Good leaders tell the followers what to expect. For instance everyone should know that the moneys available for merit increases are determined before the start of the fiscal year during the preparation of the budget. This occurs 60-90 days before the beginning of the fiscal year. Normally, a percentage of the total salary is included in the budget as a line item for merit increases. This percentage is determined in various ways. One organization we work with uses 66.7%, of the estimated CPI plus the merit portion, usually 2.5%, depending upon the competitive market. (For example, if the CPI was 3.0%, then .667*3.0% = 2.00 % plus 2.5%(merit) for a total of 4.5%) Thus, the total dollar amount for the coming budget year has been established for the total merit pool. Remember: Promotions do not come from the merit pool. Promotion increases are separately budgeted items. The recommendation becomes critical; otherwise one can get left out of consideration.

Deserve What You Get: Merit is given to recognize meritorious performance in grade; a performance which is greater than competent.

Get What you Deserve: If the performance is only competent, then one deserves only to be kept whole with respect to the 66.7% of the CPI, no more. Incidentally the reason for the 66.7% instead of 100% of the CPI is that the CPI calculation contains many items, which one does not purchase yearly and does not apply, such as a new house. Keeping whole with the living cost portion of the CPI should maintain the position pay competitive on a comparable basis, meaning that the employer would not expect to be non-competitive and loose the worker because of level of compensation.

You Get What You Earn: If your performance is below competent, do not expect even the CPI increment. Expect counseling as to how and when performance will be improved. Don't get caught in the position where "she is not bad enough to fire and not good enough to raise."

Why so Small? Merit increases, aside from the CPI slice, are generally small because the compounding of numbers will cause the salary to exceed the salary range and render the organization non-competitive. For instance, an annual increase of 10.0%, 7.0% or 5% would double the base pay in 7 years, 10 years, and 14 years, respectively. So it is important to understand the level of merit, which may be available so as not to be disappointed, or seemingly unappreciative at the amount received. Don't expect a big number for merit.

Promotions are Big: The big jumps in base pay come in the form of promotion increases. This is when one is moved from a lower pay range to a higher pay range. Generally the pay ranges are designed into 20% increment increases, i.e., there is a 20% difference from one range to the next. Now we are talking about real base pay increases. Promotion increases of 15% are not unusual.

Adequate Preparation Improves the Odds: So, before asking for the merit increase, know where you are in the present pay range. This is important. If you are below 90% of the mid-point of the pay range, then you can expect a larger merit increase and can expect some merit portion even if you are only a competent performer. If you are within the 90-110% of mid-point, known as "the middle 1/3", of the range, then competent should yield only the CPI increment. If you are above 110%, then a performance of superior or better is required to merit an increase. Competent performers seldom get promoted. Therefore, they have to be kept within the mid portion of the salary range. The superior and exceptional performers are moved up the salary range because the management knows that these are the ones who will be most likely promoted to the next salary range before she runs out of range. Guess who gets the largest piece of the merit pie? So, be sure of your performance level before you think about asking for a merit increase. Not only be sure of your performance, but also you should have been (past tense) presenting your accomplishments such that they are known not only to your immediate supervisor but also to at least the next level above. You have to sell yourself, your performance. If you have been effective in selling your performance, then you should not have to ask for a raise if you have a leader. Most of the time you will not have a good leader and will have to ask. Now, if you have done your homework, you are prepared and ready to ask for that increase in compensation. Make a reality check and go for it!

Asking for the Increase: You have information on the organization's practices and procedures with respect to compensation. You know the salary range. You know where you are located within the range. It has been X-months since your last raise. You have been doing superior work and have the evidence to substantiate it. You also know that other employees in like positions as you have received increases. Keep in mind there are no secrets with respect to compensation in an organization because salary handling violates the rule for secrecy. i.e., when more than one person knows then it is no longer a secret. You request a private audience with your supervisor. Ask for an appointment for 15 minutes in length, no more. You asked for the meeting so you should take charge by making a five-minute presentation, which hopefully will justify consideration for an increase. First, tell her the purpose is to make it easy for her to consider and recommend you for an increase. ("Tell 'em what you are going to tell 'em, then tell 'em, then tell 'em what you told 'em") Lay out the facts of your history of salary action. Compare this to the organization's practices. State your performance has been at least superior and cite several instances to justify this position, preferably written. After all you are trying to make it easy for her to recommend your increase. Don't force her to take notes to write up the justification. Summarize what you have told her and ask if she needs additional information. Ask when you might expect a reply to your request. The position has to be that you are not in begging for charity. This is a justification for something, which you truly believe you have earned. The attitude is not contrite, nor arrogant, just positive and egalitarian. If you are in fact a superior performer, the supervisor will recognize it and you will get a positive response. You may not get the raise immediately because of budget constraints. However, you should get an indication when you can expect action. If the response is anything less than this, then you may wish to examine your performance, your reality testing, and/or the capability of your supervisor. If it is the latter, then ask for a transfer from that department. Life is too short to work with a lousy supervisor. After all, the supervisor is supposed to work for you.

The Big Increases Come With Job Changes: If one is changing organizations for what appears to be a promotion, then the increase should be no less than 15% if you are unhappy in your present employment. It should be substantially greater, say, 25% to 50%, if you are happy where you are. If you are not moving up the salary ladder at the rate you should, don't be afraid to change jobs. You will likely have at least 5 career changes during your working career; so don't hang around if you are not being treated appropriately. Move it! This is discussed further in the subsequent chapter.

Salary Ranges: Job positions are surveyed either annually or every two years to determine the competitive range and are placed accordingly. The salary ranges are adjusted to keep apace with the applicable portion of the CPI. Generally this is done the earlier of when the increase totals 5.0% or greater, or every two years. Organizations do this to assure competitiveness in comparable positions, as they do not wish to lose competent or better performing employees. It is more economical to keep good employees than to hire replacements and train. Further, it is just good leadership and good management to establish the trust that management will always keep the employees pay competitive.

Postscript: Be sure to weigh all the facts before asking. Take the case of the upper manager who made a strong case for a substantial raise. He did get the raise and was shortly thereafter demassed from the organization because it was determined that the last raise had moved him over the "red line" into the category of the highly paid who were to be let go in a cost reduction move. Sometimes we lose by winning. If you have good reality testing, you will know when to ask! And, you will know when to move on.

Specific Transformation Problems

Chapter 18

FINDING ANOTHER JOB–OR THE GRASS IS ALWAYS GREENER

How do you know when to change jobs? Can we depend on such conventional axioms as: the grass is greener on the other side of the fence; the best post you ever served in was the last one; the best community you ever lived in was the one you just left, or the best job you ever will have is the one you are leaving for. Maybe! It depends! Be sure!

Typically, the new worker today can expect to have from five to seven careers during her working life. This

does not mean necessarily that she will have to change companies to change careers. The developing technology is changing so rapidly that each new technology will become obsolete within a life span of three to seven years. New technology equals a positive new career. An organization headed by a leader with a healthy personality will manage the changes in technology and constantly train the followers so they can change careers without leaving the organization. It is the humanistic thing to do. It is the economical thing to do.

We know that not all leaders have healthy personalities. When the organization's leader does not have a healthy personality, the organization will fall behind the industry curve and drift toward mediocrity. We have discussed this previously. The superior and exceptional performers leave the ship first. When you are positive that this is happening, get out. It is time to leave. How do you do it well? The following are some thoughts:

Rule 1. A bird in the hand is better than two in the bush. So, don't get mad and just quit. That is economic hara-kiri. You are a more desirable candidate if you have a job. The reasoning goes: if you are "on the street," there is a reason, and the chances are it is not a good reason. So, don't let go of the bird until you have the other one securely in hand.

Rule 2. The job hunt must not attract attention at the present place of employment. Don't let up on your performance. Do not use company facilities such as postage machines, copiers, etc., for the search. Spend a few bucks and get it done outside. This is honest. Also, this preserves confidentiality. A leak could speed your departure before you are ready. Remember, when more than one person knows, it is no longer a secret.

Rule 3. Prepare a first class resume. If you have not had recent experience in doing this and doing it well, obtain outside consultation. It is worth it. The resume is the first thing the prospective employer sees. A first class job laid out on heavy weight bond paper attracts attention and says a lot about the applicant. Make a good first impression.

Rule 4. Transmit the resume under cover of a letter to the person doing the hiring no one else. Otherwise, you are probably wasting postage. In the cover letter, state the reasons for the correspondence. In the last paragraph, state that you will call within ten days to follow up on the letter. Do it. Follow up within 7 to 10 days. Be persistent. The early bird does get the worm and so does the persistent bird.

Rule 5. Interviewing is not a natural process, so prepare well. You are not born with this ability. It is learned. Practice the process beforehand. Many outstanding people fail to get jobs because they are lousy at interviewing. Conversely, many lousy performers are hired because they are outstanding at interviewing. That is another reason we prefer use of the Rousey Assessment of Personality (RAP). The scientific approach to assessing personality complements uncertainties found in the interview factor. Practice anyway; the organization you apply to may not use the RAP. Learn as much as you can about the organization through the media, annual reports, 10Ks or employees. Relax. This is not a life and death issue, at least not yet. Remember you still have a job. Ask lots of questions. Make sure the grass is really greener.

In the final interview after you have the offer, work out the details. Provide flexibility in the starting time, as you will need to give adequate notice to your present employer. This request is seldom declined and reflects well on you.

Rule 6. How do you leave? So, you have an offer. How do you properly quit the place where you are now working? You have been dissatisfied with that supervisor who has been on your case for a very long time, and now at last the opportunity has presented itself for you to tell her just what you think about her and the organization. Resist it. Don't do it. Burned bridges are difficult to recross. The occasion may arise some day in the future that you will want to cross that bridge for some well founded reason. Be professional. You should talk with your supervisor and explain that you have been offered an opportunity which will further your career. It is an offer that you just could not turn down. You would like to give the organization two weeks notice, or, if you are deep into some complicated project which requires more than two weeks to wind down

to a point of turnover to someone else, then give more time. This is the professional thing to do. Be prepared for the supervisor to say, because of an unhealthy personality which you have experienced for some time, that you can pack up right this minute, clear out your locker or desk and leave under supervision. If this occurs, then you can feel very comfortable that you are indeed making the right move, just a little late.

Remember you are not leaving to get even. You are leaving a bad situation for a better situation. So, leave everyone in as good a humor as possible. Some organizations and people do give recommendations for years after one has departed. Things could change later, and you might want to return to the organization. So, don't temp fate, as you may be tempted to do in the "exit interview" that many organizations employ to better read the situation within the organization. Even if the senior management is interviewing you, again don't tempt fate and try to get even. Use carefully chosen words in order to leave management with the best possible opinion of you. You will gain nothing by being vindictive.

Rule 7. Handling the Recommendation: We can say that the chance for the possible bad recommendation is becoming less and less. Judgments handed down by the courts have made it unattractive for most organizations to give recommendations on past employees, particularly if it is less than a sterling recommendation. The courts have made it decidedly attractive for organizations to institute a policy of NO RECOMMENDATIONS, period. Typically, an organization will confirm that this person worked for the entity from this date to that date, no more, no less, even if the person had a sterling work record. By the way, the organization should designate only one person to handle all requests for recommendations. The risk of a lawsuit from a negative comment is too great and can be costly. Even with the law on your side, resist temptation. Don't tell them off. Leave the way you would like someone to depart if you owned the company. Besides, you may find that the grass is not really greener on the other side of the fence, and you may want to go back. It has been done. Erma Bombeck wrote a book entitled *The Grass Is Always Greener over the Septic Tank*–a nice thought to hold on to when departing.

Specific Transformation Problems

Chapter 19

LENDING COMPANY EQUIPMENT

Be careful what you lend: The trend today is for management and the technicians (or, if you will, the exempt and non-exempt) to work closer together in a non-adversarial relationship for the betterment of the organization and, therefore, of the employees. This is a natural outgrowth of the increasing egalitarianism and democratization in the work place. Several years ago, this relationship was extended to show that the company was cooperative and supportive of the employees to the extent of lending certain tools and equipment to the employees to do their domestic chores. Such generous action could have economic benefit for the employees while at the same time costing the company little or nothing. The liability laws have brought this practice into focus rather sharply as a company can be held liable for the use and the misuse of any tools or equipment lent by the company, which may bring harm to the employee or to non-employees, even if misused, or wrongly applied.

The following vignette is an example of this: Two of the maintenance people in a large company borrowed portable acetylene and oxygen tanks, torches, and tools with which to repair their home air conditioning units. In the process of the compressor repair, the oxygen tank exploded with fragments of the tank ripping into the two like an anti-personnel bomb. This explosion severed both legs of one employee and caused the loss of a leg for the second individual. Both of these employees managed to recover only because of the expert training they had received under the company's program of emergency medical training. Because of this training, one of the injured men maintained consciousness long enough to direct the spouses during the emergency in what actions to take to preserve life until the emergency personnel and equipment arrived and removed them to the hospital emergency room. Both men healed but only after a long painful recovery period. The monetary damages consisted of paying all of the medical bills, the loss of income, and a settlement in the order of several million dollars to each of the employees. The company, the company's insurance carrier, and the manufacturer of the oxygen bottle paid this. The lesson from this is that as much as you might like to befriend one of your good employees and as much as you might like to lend equipment or tools, the liability laws bring you back to the stark reality of risk vs. reward. Don't do it.

The organization cannot avoid the liability: There is no way that the company can transfer the liability for the misuse of equipment to the employee, or for the company to escape that liability. Company practice and procedure should be in writing and should state the company does not lend anything that the company owns to anyone for any purpose. The equipment and the tools of the corporation should always be used only by qualified people within the corporation for the benefit of the corporation. This may sound cold and unfriendly, but this is the only way the company can protect itself under present liability laws.

Lending sends an undesirable psychological message: Another reason for not allowing employees to take home tools or equipment is the psychological message it gives the employee. In one sense, it can be seen as a degrading or paternalistic maneuver on the part of the management to tell employees that they can take these things home because it assumes that they are incapable of procuring them on their own. It certainly doesn't encourage them to take any responsibility for developing individual responsibility or individual entrepreneurial effort. It also raises the psychological question of blurring the distinction between work and home on the part of the employee. Since most employees have a tendency to fuse or meld their identity with that of the employer, lending them the equipment further confirms that instead of working for the employer eight hours a day, they are "working" for the employer twenty-four hours a day. This behavior never really lets them have a life apart from the organization. It's almost as if they never have a vacation. They are always on duty in a psychological sense. So that quite aside from the self-serving interest of the employer of not wanting to be involved in any legal entanglements, it is also reasonable to assume that the employer is doing the employee a disservice by encouraging this kind of psychological dependence and lack of respect for them as individuals separate from the company.

Your checklist should include

Item 1. A written Practice and Procedure that prohibits the loan of company tools, equipment, and vehicles.

Item 2. A straightforward explanation to each employee why the organization has to take this seemingly unfriendly position.

Item 3. Frequent follow-up to assure the Practice and Procedure is active and is being followed to the letter.

Your insurance carriers will applaud you and should lower your rates.

Specific Transformation Problems

Chapter 20

WHEN TO CUT COSTS AND WHEN TO SPEND

When to cut costs and when to spend: Most people approach a crisis transformation believing that all they have to do is to reduce costs by reducing the number of

employees and cutting back on services. They apparently believe that this approach will solve their problems. The belief that you can save yourself into prosperity is frequently misguided, as it will not achieve the transformation. There is a time when it is necessary to cut costs, and there is a time when it is necessary to spend.

Costs should be reduced and maintained at their lowest effective level. However, you should be very cautious after the fat in the organization has been removed. Remove only the fat; make sure that the muscle is not being removed.

Reducing people vs. improving efficiency: In most organizations, especially industrial process type organizations, the people costs are usually 5-7% of the total cost. A 20% reduction in this cost yields a 1.0-1.4% in the total cost. A 1.0 to 1.4% increase in overall organization efficiency accomplishes the same result. This is not meant to imply that cost reduction should not be a constant goal; it should. When a company reduces costs by $1.00, this entire amount falls to the pretax line. Taxes take approximately 50% and $0.50 remains as profit. To accomplish the same profit impact, by increasing sales the company must increase sales by $20 if the pretax margin is 5% on sales. Or, say, the P/E (price/earnings) ratio is 20 to 1.0. The equity value of the company is increased by $10.00 dollars for each $1.00 pretax cost reduction. This can be a significant contributor to the addition of economic value. If you are not adding economic value to the entity, then you are reducing the value to the shareholders.

The leverage for saving is such that constant monitoring of costs by an effective cost control system is a vital management responsibility. The goal is to always have the lowest cost for what is produced. This assures cost competitiveness and survival. The lowest cost will be the last survivor, even if you manufacture buggy whips. Again, you do not save yourself into prosperity. They market themselves into prosperity and marketing requires spending money to make money. A good, well thought out strategic plan will indicate those areas where dollars should be spent and those areas in which costs can and should be controlled either by reduction or the complete elimination of unnecessary and/or unprofitable functions. The old saying that if you build a better mousetrap, the world will beat a path to your door only applies to those who have superior marketing. Technology itself does not sell. Only marketing sells.

Check the leverage of spending: The dilemma of when to spend and when to save is illustrated by the November 1, 1993, *New York Times* article by Mr. Keith Bradsher with the headline "Trade Office Called Too Tiny to Achieve International Goals." Mr. Bradsher writes, "When negotiators with the office of the United States Trade Representative planned a trip to Japan last year, they had to choose between taking a lawyer or a translator because their travel budget was too small for both. When the Trade Representative, Mickey Kantor, flew to Brussels in March, he slept in coach class because of the limited money for travel.

When the Bush Administration's Agriculture Secretary, Edward R. Madigan, left a working dinner of consommé and finger sandwiches given by the trade representative's office last fall, he complained to reporters: "We've just been treated to an evening repast by U.S.T.R. Now we're going to get something to eat." Stepping into his limousine, Mr. Madigan added, "U.S.T.R. is a very low-budget operation". Mr. Madigan was right. At a time when unprecedented emphasis is being given to trade issues, American trade policy was being run on a shoestring.

Leaving politics aside for the moment, it is clear that a critical office with a budget of $20 million per year to deal with billions and billions of dollars of trade opportunities is trying to save expense dollars when the emphasis should be clearly upon return. The issue should be what is the return for the spending of one incremental dollar. What is the advantage for spending one more dollar? The cheapest may not be the most economical.

There are no really hard and fast rules as to when cutting costs should dominate over increased spending.

Manage the Personality–Not the Person

This is a matter of judgment based upon a sound, well-developed, and well thought out strategic plan for transforming the process.

Government change is difficult: It is virtually impossible to reduce the bureaucratic costs in government although it is the correct financial option to exercise. It is impossible to implement because of the politics. Any time a governmental program is reduced, someone's ox is being gored. The structure of special interest groups has made it impossible to gore anyone's ox without loud raucous noises being raised over the countryside. Contrast that with business where the sole criterion is or should be economic analysis. It is government's responsibility, not business, to deal with social issues.

Economics drives business changes: Business exists primarily for one reason: to make a profit. Therefore, no other logical reason should come into play whenever deciding whether a particular cost, function, or service should be reduced or eliminated. Does it make business sense? Does it increase economic value? The primary consideration must be an economic one.

Don't reduce the headcount unless you change the way things are done: Reducing the number of people in the organization is not a long-term solution unless the process is changed. Change the way things are done to achieve efficiencies, then the personnel reductions will stick. Otherwise, the number of employees in an organization will creep back up to and frequently greater than the level before reduction was initiated. Frequently the "creep-back" in employee count is disguised as consultants for top management's benefit.

One can challenge the process without direct confrontation. Every company has too many reports that are prepared by too many people. Too many people must read said reports once prepared. This consumes time and energy, which could be applied more effectively elsewhere in the organization. If you face this situation, try this without comment. Eliminate a report, wait, and see how many readers complain and lobby for reinstatement. This works very well as a weeding process. It is fast, does not require a committee, prompts fast feedback, can be easily corrected with minimum effort, and avoids the wasted hours for a detailed study. If nothing else comes from the exercise, you can almost guarantee that the number of copies will be reduced and the volume of content reduced to only the essential data required for those who really have to know. It is not necessary for an organization to eliminate positions in order to become more efficient.

Shareholder value vs. social services: The previous statement may be construed as being in conflict with our philosophy of the humanistic treatment of employees. One should remember that corporate America is not in the social services business. Again, business exists to create shareholder value. The dealing with social problems and related issues must remain the sole domain of the various branches of governments, local, state and federal. Economic situations will require corporate reductions to manage costs. This translates into the elimination of people and/or a change of process. However, this can be and should be done in the most humanistic way possible. We have already discussed how to terminate the right way and how to terminate the wrong way in cases where it is necessary to discharge people because of changes in market or changes in cost structure. This latter circumstance seems to impose a special obligation upon the management. It is a moral obligation because this type of situation is usually generated due to less than optimum strategic planning or execution of the plan, rather than the work product, per se. The obligation is a requirement of the organization to provide outplacement services and all reasonable assistance possible to help these employees cope with their new situation, financially and psychologically.

Corporate citizen: The distinction should be made between the corporation avoiding the social engineering business or avoiding being involved in the business of correcting the perceived societal ills of the day versus that of being a good corporate citizen. The corporation always has the obligation and responsibility to be a good corporate citizen, to cooperate with the local community, to communicate effectively with them and to encourage its employees to be active participants within the affairs and governance of the local community. The business of correcting the social inequities that exist in our modern day society is best addressed by the government entities and supported by the taxes that the corporation and its employees pay for these and other purposes.

Miscellaneous Transformation Issues

Chapter 21

EGALITARIANISM

Webster's New Collegiate Dictionary describes ***egalitarianism*** as "a belief in human equality especially with respect to social, political, and economic rights and privileges." Egalitarianism will be the mode of the early 2000s. Everyone wants more control over his or her working conditions. We are not willing to knowingly subjugate ourselves, or to lessen our sense of value in relation to anyone else regardless of rank or position. We want more control over our lives, which translates into more control over our work. This is good. It is different. It is tough to manage. We have stated previously that no one has the right, although they may have the power, to knowingly do anything either directly or indirectly or by insinuation or by position that will lessen the self-esteem of another individual. Therefore, the task in corporate America is to manage these large numbers of equals who are striving for democratization in the work place. Can we do this using the old management tools of the 1960s, 70s, and 80s? That is the challenge. We don't think so.

Managerial structures–non-collective bargaining: If one takes a hard look at the managerial structures that are in place in many organizations, one has to seriously question whether or not such structures can effectively manage these large groups of "equals" over the long term. This question has to be asked, particularly, if you have a non-union work place. We believe that the best management structure is the hierarchical structure. This type of organization provides structure and clearly delineates responsibility and authority. The autocratic hierarchy works only if the leader is a benevolent dictator. In the autocracy one person has unlimited power. It has been said that power corrupts and absolute power corrupts absolutely. The preferred structure is the hierarchy with empowered ranks. The power is delegated by definition to the ranks by each subordinate to the one above it. You might think of this type of hierarchical structure as an empowered autocracy. Readers acquainted with the proposals of E. Jacque will see some similarity to his theory of how to manage.

Manage the Personality-Not the Person

Managerial structure–collective bargaining: Autocracy works in the unionized work place because in union shops people are managed not as individuals but as a large monolithic group of individuals who are represented by the union steward of the collective bargaining unit. This type of managing requires a different approach, a different thought process and a different value system than the non-bargaining unit. In union shops the rules, regulations, and procedures are all laid out in the negotiated contract with the union. Therefore, the responsibilities and requirements for managing the collective bargaining entity are completely different from those required for managing the non-collective bargaining entity. Management does not have to consider each person as an individual with equal rights and privileges and equal say. It is all spelled out in the negotiated contract. Union is singular, not plural. A member of the union is a part of the singular entity and managed as such. The union leader wants it this way as it assures control and continued flow of dues. Most people who belong to unions probably are not interested in democratization of the work place or they would not subjugate themselves to the dictates of the union boss and pay dues for this privilege of lack of individualism. They need structure. This is supported by our observation that

80% of the population require structure. It is believed that most union members are members not only because of the structure provided, but because they believe membership provides job security and guarantees fair compensation. Unions have been reasonably successful in trading on the above personality requirements by providing extensive structure. Still the real drawing card for the union has been job security, the ultimate sales pitch.

Providing structure: Who is in a better position to provide structure than the company? If you believe that 80% of the population requires structure, then one can readily conclude that if the organization--be it plant, school, hospital, or other--does not provide the needed structure, then some other entity will step in to fill that need. Someone must cater to and provide this personality necessity. In the absence of such action by the organization, the union organizer steps in. We advance the thesis that unions have lost in total membership the past decade because their structure suppressed the growing need for egalitarianism and individuality. Some persons in management have begun to wake up to the needs of the individual.

Right to know: The 2000s are bringing forth the requirement that the employee be listened to and treated as an individual. This is a reasonable and appropriate request because if you invest your working life with a corporation, you have a right to know what is going on in that corporation. You have a right to know if the corporation is prospering or not prospering. You have a right to know the corporation's position on social issues, on environmental issues and on anything that could impact the company and thus impact the career of the individual. Yes, we are advocating that employees at all levels have a right to know any information that may impact their working career as a quid pro quo for their depreciating a non-renewable asset, their working years, for the corporate entity.

Right to be heard: They also have a right to be heard. They have a right to honest dialogue and intellectual honesty. There is an effort being made to do this in several ways in corporations from copying the Japanese pattern of quality circles to holding meetings on a regular basis for people to raise questions and voice their concerns and obtain answers from management. All of these actions increase an individual's self esteem and makes them feel less helpless.

Right to communicate, not to "bitch": A word of caution is that one should guard against permitting these group meetings from turning into "bitch" sessions for particular individuals to bring very specific and personal complaints. It is believed that no one employee has the right to impose a five-minute harangue, which has a singular application, on other employees. The company should have a procedure which permits individual issues to naturally flow up through the organization and, if need be, all the way to the CEO in order to get them resolved rather than bringing them up at company wide meetings. People have to believe they will not be punished for honest and valid dissent. This form of challenge clarifies and adds credibility to the message.

Set personality boundaries: Again with reference to prohibiting an employee from spending five minutes talking about their own personal problems, one needs to recognize that this rule or limit setting does create boundaries for the employee. An employee who talks about personal problems loses sight of the individual boundaries they have *vis a vis* the other employees as well as the organization. This loss of reality testing needs to be contained. The only way you can contain it is by providing structure. It is not that these problems are not real to the person, obviously they are. But, as previously discussed, management needs to have some other way for this to be heard in the organization. Open dialogue will solve most but not all of these real and perceived problems. Many employee issues and problems are clearly beyond the purview of management and should be referred to external specialists. For the more difficult issues, an employee assistance program, (EAP), can often be an ideal outlet.

Stay within the boundaries: Another issue that comes to mind in terms of the preceding discussion is the importance for management not to get caught up in terms of reacting inappropriately or negatively to the employee during these sessions. This can occur if the input of the employee is terminated prematurely or the manager reacts as if the anger is directed toward them rather than the company policy. Thus, it is important for them to separate out their self and feelings from what is being said. In reality the employee who talks on for five minutes without realizing it is inappropriate and the manager/leader who gets upset with the employee and tries to stifle their discussion are really two sides of the same coin. Both of them have lost their boundaries of what is really happening in the situation.

Obligation and responsibility: At the risk of being misunderstood, the right to be heard does not equate to the right to govern. The responsibility of governance ultimately rests with the leader. Remember responsibility and the authority has to go always hand in hand. You just cannot give a person the responsibility without the authority to carry out that responsibility. However, the obligation for the employee body to be heard carries with it the obligation of management to fairly and equitably consider the feedback and then, to either act upon this feedback, or to explain in a comprehensible fashion why certain actions were or were not taken. It should be noted that older employees have a tendency to become more skeptical faster than the younger employees do if their ideas are not implemented. Thus, great care should be exercised with the groups to explain the reasons why a suggestion was or, more importantly, was not used.

Management's response: Moving from skepticism to cynicism on the part of an employee is a sign that management has offered an explanation not consistent with reality. Management's response cannot be perceived to be threatening. It must be understood as honest and straightforward. This is only practicing the Golden Rule and dealing with these issues in a humanistic fashion.

Why not ask the experts? Another challenge facing corporations today is the significant downsizing that is being required in many cases in order to be competitive on a worldwide basis. This has removed many of the choices and many the excess bureaucratic structures that were believed to be necessary in order to maintain "control" of the employee body. It is slowly but surely becoming recognized that the one person who knows the most about the job being done and how it can be done most efficiently and most effectively is the employee who occupies the 35 square feet of space in which she work eight hours a day.

Management is finally concluding that neither they, nor their engineering, financial or other staff departments have all the answers. Increasingly they are going to the individual on the floor or in the plant and asking them, "If you were the King of France, or if you were the CEO with the responsibility of running this company, what would you

do to make your job more effective? What would you change so it might be done more efficiently and at the same time provide greater satisfaction to you in performing the task? What would you do to get a greater psychic kick from your job?"

One result is that these workers, or these associates, are first, surprised and frequently suspicious at being asked after all these years of management's practiced silence in this regard. Management is equally surprised when these workers willingly and enthusiastically provide a well articulated series of suggestions as to how things can be done better and more effectively for the benefit of themselves (i.e., provide more psychic enjoyment from the job) as well as added benefits for the corporation.

This practice of asking, if effectively carried out can be the first step in moving a corporation toward greater egalitarianism democratization. We all wish to be heard. We want dialogue. We want to be important. We want our ideas to be recognized. We want to enjoy our work. And why shouldn't the person closest to the task be asked and then listened to? And responded to? After all, these are the same people who volunteer for the local city government, the little league baseball, sit on the boards of trustees of schools and churches, run committees, fund raising, solicit for all sorts of community causes, organize community activities and manage households. All of these non-company activities involve very complex human relations that develop and hone the personal qualities of the individual.

Manage the Personality-Not the Person

Who are the dumb people in your organization? Why should management believe that these people suddenly go dumb when they walk through the front gate of a plant or the door of the office? While management may recognize this from a cerebral analysis, the actions and practices by management in most companies treat these employees as if they suddenly go dumb when they walk into the work place. Therefore, industry has built up supervisory and bureaucratic structures to closely monitor and manage these individuals.

Who said that Theory X management is dead? It is unnecessary, inefficient, and redundant. The best way to solve this is to dialogue with these people, bring them into the process, and make them an integral part of the decision process. In so doing you will find that they do not have to be monitored and measured constantly. They are quite capable of making decisions even at the entry levels of employment. Management must be open, management must be trusting, and management must provide them sufficient information. Management must encourage and help them apply their reasoning capabilities and experiences outside of work to issues and problems they face on the job.

Miscellaneous Transformation Issues

Chapter 22

THE GOLDEN RULE

What is generally referred to as The Golden Rule is another way for handling and preventing problems. Doing unto others as we would have them do unto us is a very practical and a very necessary rule that should be employed by the leader/manager and by the technician. The key here is that in any given situation if one can place themselves in the position of the other party and say how would I like to be treated if I were in that person's position, then we can avert most of the difficulties that occur within our organizations. It is critical to see the world through the other person's eyes and in so doing we can better temper our responses and our reactions so we can provide a more humanistic response and a more pleasant working environment.

Don't confuse power and right. No one has the right, although they may have the power, to do anything to another human being, which will lessen that person's self esteem. The understanding that has to be attained is that the manager/leader works for the employees. They are not "her people"; she is theirs. The manager/leader serves the followers. The true leader is a servant of the followers.

So again, one should be reminded that the Golden Rule is called "golden" for good reason. If we can remember to treat the other person the way we would like to be treated, then we can avoid these pitfalls by making the work environment "golden."

Miscellaneous Transformation Issues

Chapter 23

SELF-ESTEEM & THE HOSTILITY TRAP

Power Corrupts: One of the problems which management has with newly coined supervisors is that they suddenly become "intoxicated" with this newfound power of being a supervisor and having domain over the area and the people under their supervision. This can become a very difficult situation if the supervisor is someone with a personality problem. Further complicating the situation are features such as the new supervisor never having been counseled, coached or trained for their new responsibilities. Typically, the supervisor will use this newfound authority to impose his will upon the supervised without adequate communication; without feedback. As a result he will depreciate or lessen this person's self esteem. Whenever one lessens another person's self esteem, for whatever reason, they throw that person into the hostility trap. This person becomes hostile. They become hostile at the individual, they will become hostile at the corporation and they really can become hostile at the world. The new supervisor has just moved one of the 18% group to the 2% group.

Lessen Self-Esteem, Increase Hostility: The fact that the individual who's self esteem has been lessened becomes hostile makes some sense if one stops to think about it. Whenever one's persona is attacked, the person is going to defend himself simply as a matter of self-preservation. You have basically two choices of defending yourself. You can either run (flight) or you can resist (fight). In the case of the person who chooses to run, this person would lose the job, which would really be totally maladaptive. To become hostile would help serve the same instinct even though it is in one sense also maladaptive. The point is that in the act of reducing one's self-esteem the person is threatened. Hostility should be an expected outcome of a supervisor denigrating an associate.

Don't Get Mad, Get Even: It is worthwhile to remember that a hostile employee can always get even. They can get even with the supervisor or the company. Frequently instead of going directly at the supervisor they will get even with the company as a way of satisfying their anger or their hostility. There is no way any corporation can guard against this type of response. The only answer, or certainly the most logical answer, is to take the steps necessary to avoid the hostility in the first place. Don't add to the 2%.

An example of this is the case of a marketing entity where two young college graduates had been hired at the same time and together had gone through the training program of this company. When it came time to promote one of these to the first level of supervision, management chose the one who they thought was obviously the most qualified. However, management not too tactfully explained to the other one why he wasn't chosen and lessened this person's self-esteem. This person chose not to run. Instead the person chose to stay and fight. He didn't get mad; he decided to get even with the company.

He determined precisely what the dollar amount for the promotion was for the other person, approximately $48.50 a month. He felt that he was had been wronged and was rightly due the promotion and the increase that should have accompanied it. So for the next twenty-five years this person very systematically took this amount of money from the company every month. He kept detailed records for all these years. Finally after twenty-five years the company's auditors picked up the missing $48.50/month and confronted this person. Interestingly, there was neither guilt nor shame on this person's part whatsoever. He felt that he was absolutely justified regarding his actions which he had taken as he proudly delivered from his garage the complete records for twenty-five years of precisely how it was done, when it was done, etc. This is a case where the employee didn't get mad, he just got even. The employee always has the last say when it comes to getting even with the company.

Child - Adult – Child: The reader who has children will immediately correlate this example with the actions of a young child. That is, if a child feels they are denied cookies, or a toy, a two or three-year-old will do something to get back at the parent and get even. This is the level of the behavior illustrated by the above employee who was not promoted. Thus, there is a corollary between the behavior of the employee and the young child.

Miscellaneous Transformation Issues

CHAPTER 24

MIND THE DETAILS

Details vs. micro managing: Minding the details requires walking a very fine line between getting too involved in the details and being accused of micro

managing. The other choice is macro managing and being accused of completing ignoring the details. Ignore the details and the project will fail. The key is to be able to differentiate the important details from the unimportant. Back to reality testing again. In any given set of information that flows over the desk of any employee, 80%

of the data is not critical. In fact, a significant part of the data is unimportant, and a surprising amount is totally unnecessary. The challenge for the employee, supervisor, manager, and the leader is to be able to process all of the information that flows to them and decide effectively and efficiently what is important and what is not important. To be effective and efficient in this endeavor, you should have a clear vision and be able to differentiate between those things that you can affect and those things over which you exercise neither control nor influence. It is helpful if you will take the time to list those things you can change and those you cannot change. This speeds up the filtering or screening of data. The explosion of information can overwhelm and inundate if you are not able to establish priorities for time management. This filtering will guide you on the amount of time that should be spent on further analysis. This same attention to important detail applies in performing a task as well as analyzing data.

For instance it was pointed out to me many, many years ago when running a projector in a movie theater that threading the film through the projector was really not as complicated as the instruction book appeared to make it. That is, there were really only two critical details that should be observed: (1) be sure to put a large loop before the lens' entrance and (2) have a large loop after the lens' exit. Otherwise, the projector would skip frames and ultimately the film would break. That was a very simple but memorable lesson. One well remembers what happens when the film breaks at a critical moment in the movie. Not only does the theater go dark, but also a perfectly normal placid audience can become verbal and sometimes abusive. Always look for the most critical detail and then the second most important detail. Remember that 80% of the details are just that–details–and relatively unimportant. Focus on the goal, and don't get caught up in the process.

Thoughts become habits: Management data fall into largely the same category because one has to deal with a whole series of reports or information that may flow across one's workspace. The important things will be 1) look at the bottom line, 2) look at the yields, and then 3) look at the efficiencies. If those all line up, you know that, everything has to fall in line. This type of thought process will develop the actions that become habits, which in turn will permit you to function at your efficient best. The issue of minding the important details is believed to be a training issue as much as a personality issue, although we should take care not to underestimate the vital role of the personality.

Recognition Leads to Time Management: The issue of data screening falls into the same category as time management and probably should be part of that training. With the proliferation of computers that yields more and more data, you need to develop this discipline. The whole explosion of information is coming at all of us at such a rate that it is literally impossible to pay attention to all of the details even if we wished to do so. So, it is very important to differentiate those items that are controlling from those that are the cues to indicate that further analysis is required and determine if additional time should be expended. An example of this would be the typical multi-page daily production reports from an operating plant. These and many other reports like the cash report, the cash analysis, etc., cross the desk of the manager with uncommon regularity. The key item in the daily production report that you can quickly scan is the production for the last twenty-four hours. If that is equal to or greater than the programmed or the budgeted rate, then you move immediately to look at the inventory levels to see if those are moving up or down from the previous day. That gives a clear indication as to whether or not budgeted shipments were made. You don't have to move to see what was shipped. Look at the inventory. If it is lower than it was the day before and the plant produced at the budgeted rate, then you know the plant shipped more than was produced. That is good; no need to move on and dig through all of shipping numbers.

What is Key? In our example of a particular chemical plant, the percentage of hydrogen gives an indication of the overall efficiency. If that is below a given number, then the efficiency is very good. If it is a high number, then it says to back up and look at more detail to determine what is causing the inefficiency.

The review of the daily cash flow analysis is another good indicator. You look at one quick number and it indicates how much investment was made and how that compares to yesterday's investment. Is it showing an increase or decrease? Then you can do a serial comparison. It is all on the same page. You can see very quickly what has happened the past week. If cash is increasing, then you know that billings and collections are on a reasonable basis and there is cash to operate. Businesses live or die depending upon their cash flows. No need to look at the details such as individual payments and to whom, etc. The review of large volumes of data can be simplified and the review time greatly reduced if you will take the time to understand the keys while keeping in mind those things that you can change. There is always a key piece of information within the data that will tell you whether you need to scrutinize the next level of information. This process can lead you quickly and effectively through the data reviews without sitting and poring over the entire list, item by item. This is effective; this is efficient. This is reality.

Key Details: Minding the key details is very important to the crisis transformation manager and to the manager who is in a constant transformation situation. If you monitor *all* the details, you fail. If you ignore the details, you fail. In contrast, minding the key details optimizes management time and your time for managing. In a constant transformation operation, the senior manager would not be monitoring details to the extent required for a crisis transformation. Once a level operation has been established with a very predictable situation, then the responsibility of monitoring can be delegated to at least the next level, and possibly further down for review and corrective action depending upon the extent of defined empowerment in the organization.

Manage by exception: If there is a key point outside of "the normal, plus or minus" operating range, the designated responsible person would have the obligation to advise that it is off plan and indicate the actions taken to return to plan. This is managing by exception. The transition from information monitoring in a crisis transformation to that of monitoring in a constant transformation mode or managing by exception, does not show up suddenly on one bright morning as the rooster crows. The decision that we will no longer be monitoring this or we will no longer be supporting this as of a certain date is not made suddenly or crisply. It just doesn't happen this way. Experience indicates that this type of monitoring and follow through is reduced on an incremental basis based upon the performance of the people down the line as they empower themselves. This will vary from supervisor to supervisor, from manager to manager, and especially from CEO to CEO, depending upon how comfortable he feels.

Assuming empowerment: Move the decision-making down to the lowest practical level in the organization. The empowerment of people is an incremental process that begins to move decision-making down the organization's hierarchy with the ultimate goal of finally getting it down to the individuals who are actually running the plant. It is not the first line supervisors, but ultimately the operators who have assumed empowerment to take actions within preset parameters to keep the operation at the desired operating level and efficiencies. When the development has effectively reached this state of empowerment, the first line of supervision as we know it today becomes redundant.

This is like deciding when to give the car keys to your adolescent child, whom you have been training, coaching, supporting, and supervising. Although you may never feel totally comfortable, there is some point when it is "the right time," and you hand over the keys. This doesn't come on a specific predetermined day. It depends on the performance and how well these functions have been carried out and demonstrated. It is "gut" check time. If it doesn't feel right, don't do it. You make this grand decision with great trepidation and hand over the keys while offering a silent prayer with your fingers crossed. If it works well, then the next time the task of trusting empowerment is easier. Vindication of your judgment by positive feedback reinforces your self-confidence in decision-making.

Miscellaneous Transformation Issues

Chapter 25

LISTENING – A LEARNED ART

Listen to Persuade: Listening is a learned art. There are four stages required for successful listening...the first stage is **phatic**, which *Webster's New Collegiate Dictionary* defines as coming .. "from the Greek word *phatos*.. revealing or sharing feelings or establishing an atmosphere of sociability rather than communicating ideas". This is the small talk that takes place when one first meets another person...where you live, what schools you attended, the business you are in, type of work, etc...all those small details which permits one to size up the person's background for some degree or level of commonality.

When one becomes comfortable at that level then the relationship moves to the second stage: **cathartic**, which *Webster* defines as "of, relating to, or producing catharsis". Catharsis also means "to cleanse, purge". This is the stage where one feels comfortable enough with the relationship to be able to "dump" or become cathartic and talk about more intimate things and to safely inquire about more intimate details of the person. A level of trust and credibility has developed in the relationship. You have to get close enough and trust the other person enough to be vulnerable.

Now and only now, is the relationship ready for the third stage: **information**. Information can now be passed and will be listened to and heard. Before this time, the parties were not sure they could trust anything the other party may pass to them and if you can't trust it then why spend a lot of effort listening.

So, the phatic and the cathartic stages have to be successfully accomplished before any meaningful information can be passed. Then and only then, can the relationship move to the fourth stage: **persuasion**. Now, and only now, is one ready to sell or convince the other party. Good communicators know this, good listeners know this. Good salesmen practice this. Good Leaders make it a habit.

Is Perception Truth? How many people do you know who really truly say exactly what they mean? The authors would venture a bet, that you could count the number of acquaintances on one hand and then have some fingers left, who do in fact "tell it like it is". People do not resort to such behavior because they are liars. They don't do it because they are bad. They are not liars. They are nice, hard working people who mean well. Further, they would never knowingly and consciously tell a lie. They honestly think they are speaking the truth. That is their perception. They would be horrified to think that anyone, let alone a fellow worker, ever thought they were other than truthful. Deciphering what is meant in a work or personal situation becomes crucial to effective leadership and interacting with others. The following examples will illustrate the psychological importance for management to listen.

Example One: An example of this inability to understand what was really meant took place during a turnaround situation in a company in which certain functions were being upgraded by adding more experienced people. The situation was further complicated by the fact that the supervisor had returned as the department head after an absence "at greener pastures" which turned out not to be so green. He returned and replaced the acting department head, a woman. She had been offered the permanent position as department head. However, she

turned it down saying that she lacked the required experience. This was, for her, a brave act and great display of superior reality testing. It should be noted that she ran the department for six months at a most difficult time for the company and worked with the CEO and the Board of Directors in a competent manner. She, being a good team worker, accepted the move from acting head to section head and accordingly moved from the larger enclosed office of the department head to the section head cubical.

Shortly after this the department head returned. He began to organize and re-organize the department for greater efficiency and effectiveness and to reestablish his authority. He subsequently hired another section head, a male worker with whom he had previously worked. In fact, they were good friends of long standing. This new section head was very experienced and very capable. The process of interviewing and hiring this new section head took several weeks and quite properly involved the female section head in the interviewing and the evaluation process. This involvement clearly caused her concern and decidedly gnawed at her self-esteem. The reading between the lines by her actions and comments seemed to cry out "am I still important to the company?" She volunteered to move from the larger cubicle in favor of the new section head. Unfortunately, the department head heard only the words

and did not hear the meaning of "am I still important". He took up her offer and moved the new section head into her cubicle. She was moved to a smaller accountant's cubicle.

Unfortunately, size of the office space is still utilized to indicate rank, not space requirement. She was devastated. She came into the CEO's office to be reassured that she was still important to the company. Life would be so much simpler if people said what they mean and mean what they say.

The supervisor did not understand that she was really asking him if she was important to him and to the company. This was critical to her self-esteem, particularly with a new person, a male, coming on the scene. After all she had single-handedly carried the department for six months and did she not deserve some recognition? If she was important then, why was she not important now? She had been silently begging her supervisor to say "no" to her offer and thus let the office personnel and her know that she was important, valued and loved.

Perception Becomes Truth and Truth Becomes Reality: The supervisor being from an ethnic background, which traditionally holds the males in higher esteem than females and thus generally had lesser sensitivity to female feelings, failed to hear the meaning of what occurred. Instead he took a pragmatic action based upon what was said rather than what was meant. This was damaging to the self-esteem of a valued employee but also sent a message to all of the females in the office that this supervisor believes that the males in the office are more important than females and will be given preferential treatment.

At least this was the perception. It should be noted that perception is more important than facts because if a person or persons perceive something to be true, then this perception often becomes truth and truth becomes reality. Therefore it becomes critical to review any decision to determine as best one can as to what the perception in a situation could and most likely will be. One cannot rely on the facts because they do not always equate to perception. In any event, the perception was that he gave the appearance of giving special favors to an old friend.

Lesson One: After the smoke had cleared, an opportunity came up to discuss the situation with the department head. He was told what he had done and what the reaction had been by the displaced section head as well as the other females in the office. He was defensive to the extent of saying that she had offered the larger cubicle not once, but twice. He did understand after discussion that it was the search for approbation that fostered the offer and certainly not the belief that a male deserved better treatment than a female of equal rank. He was further advised that he had dug himself a hole as far as the female workers in the office were concerned and that he would have to be very sensitive to their feelings and would need to extract himself from this perception that his actions had created. We discussed the personalities involved and how one should be sensitive to the needs of each personality. After all, we do, like it or not, manage the personality, and we manage it one person at a time, dealing with each unique personality and unique needs. The leader must nurture his flock.

It was suggested that even if he had intended to move the new section head to the larger cubicle, it might have been better received if it had been done at a later date after the "new kid on the block" had demonstrated his superior skill and value. It also helps to talk things through and to give them time to be accepted by all of the parties

before acting. This can be a very effective form of consensus building.

Knowledge is not Operational: A logical question for the inquisitive reader at this point could be, "why didn't the supervisor of the department head, who saw this developing, stop the action?" This could have saved the further damage to the self-esteem of the female in question. It could have kept the department head out of trouble with the other females in the office. It would not, however, taught the lesson which had to be learned. And that lesson is: **knowledge is not operational.** To stop it before the experience would have provided only knowledge. The experience was required to be operational. However, it is doubtful that it would have provided the proof required to overcome the imbedded environmental value system in this supervisor relative to the value of males. No, it is not operational until one has experienced it and done it. The passage of knowledge is very helpful and it satisfies the intellectual need but deprives one of the emotional experience to sear on the brain the incident and the lesson or lessons learned. This principle is similar to the same principle used in effective psychotherapy teaching. That is, one can talk about feelings and gain an intellectual understanding, but one cannot really change feelings until they have been experienced. This particular rock in his bag had to be examined.

This incident also served another useful purpose of making the staff aware of the need to make sure that not only does one not discriminate, but one must also make sure there is no appearance of discrimination in any shape or form. Not only as pure as Caesar's wife but also the appearance of being as pure as Caesar's wife. To reiterate the lesson: very few people have the personality and self-confidence to come straight at you, you must hear what they say, but more importantly you must listen very carefully to what they mean. Analyze the personality, dctermine the needs, and react to those needs in a responsible, caring and loving way. Let people know they are important, to you and to the company.

Example Two: Another example of human behavior which may manifest itself in other than the obvious can be seen in the case of the person who was hired by a company in the position of a manager. This person had been caught up in one of these now well documented demassings of a large corporation after having been employed by this company in a middle management position for a period of many years. This person had been out of work for over a year. He had an excellent work record. However, this constant searching for a job had obviously taken a toll on his emotional health in the form of decreased self-esteem. The impact of this emotional assault was manifest in the fact that this employee even after being with the new company for a period of over a year and having received two promotions to more responsible jobs still exhibited a reluctance to assume even the normal amount of risk which one would normally expect at this level. A less experienced manager could interpret this as a form of permanent deficiency in the person's capability. However, a more sophisticated look into this person's background and an analysis of this person's personality profile made it obvious that his behavior was a direct result of issues that were caused by his extended period of unemployment and, therefore, would be of temporary duration.

Lesson Two: Another way of looking at this employee's behavior is to think of the significance of the meaning of what he was trying to communicate by saying that he couldn't do this job or couldn't do that job. Clearly one interpretation of what he was saying is that he felt incapable or impotent to do this job. Why would an otherwise capable, well-trained employee act this way? Especially one who had received two quick promotions. It certainly is quite possible that he was acting because of his fear that if he took risks in doing the job and failed because

of the risks taken that he again would be dismissed and out of a job again. In essence he would be back to his previous stage of feeling impotent, helpless and less of a man than otherwise. It is a reasonable assumption that one of the psychological feelings, men especially may have with being out of work is that they feel impotent.

The "Castrated" Employee: While this phenomena may be a reflection of a troubled society that we have in times of increased unemployment, none the less, it is a valid issue to consider in any situation where an employee is hired who has been out of work for an extended period. Even the employee who hasn't been out of work who is taking their first job is bound to feel some degree of anxiety about their performance (potency) when they go into a new kind of work situation. Thus, effort should be made on the part of the supervisor to both demonstrate and assure the employee that taking responsibility will not result in their being "castrated" or losing their job. This kind of employee is going to require some time and some patience on the part of the employer until they get through the trauma they experienced being out of work. It is as if the employee needs a corrective kind of emotional experience. This doesn't imply that the employee is psychiatrically ill or needs psychological help. It implies that the employer (the environment) needs to help the employee go through a re-living, re-educational kind of experience that they are worthy, they are potent, they are valuable, they are strong and what they do is important to the employer.

Example Three: Another example of looking at least one step behind the action to determine the psychological cause, is illustrated by the case of a woman who refused to participate in the setting of annual objectives in a company's MBO program. The outward excuse provided to her supervisor was the company's MBO program. The outward excuse provided to her supervisor was: "Why should I set objectives? After all, this is really what we are paid to do, therefore, we shouldn't have to do this because it is unfair as far as the Company is concerned."

She felt strongly that she should not participate in it. To drive the point home, the supervisor let that go by. At the end of the year this was the only employee in the Management By Objectives ("MBO") program who did not receive a cash award. When the time came for the MBOs to be set for the following year, again, the same excuse was given, i.e., after all since you are being paid why indulge in this. After talking with the employee and exploring some of the reasons it became rather obvious that this employee had this sense of fear of failure because of a distasteful personal experience which she had gone through only two years before. It became obvious that she had consciously or unconsciously concluded that if she didn't set mileposts along the road by which to be measured, then no one could accuse her of failing. It was pointed out that this was, in effect, negative goal setting which could influence her positive goals and in effect doom her to failure. Further, this particular thing was complicated by the fact that this person felt she was a failure having going through an unwanted divorce, which she perceived had been imposed upon her by a male. This specter of male control and dominance was another reason for her great reluctance.

Lesson Three: Having a complete evaluation of her personality profile, management counseled this employee and was able to convince her that she should confront these perceived issues in a positive manner. Based on the learning that occurred she did reconsider and went on to participate fully in the setting and achieving of goals in the company's MBO program.

Miscellaneous Transformation Issues

Chapter 26

KEEP SCORE OR DON'T PLAY THE GAME

Keep Score and I Will Play: We North Americans are an interesting lot of people. We are a melting pot of many ethnic tribes and a blend of many cultures. Nevertheless, we have many commonalties and characteristics that span

all of our ethnic differences. One that every leader, manager and supervisor should be aware of.... is that people will play any game so long as they can keep score. No one wants to play if one cannot readily determine if they are winning or losing. Playing a game without keeping score is like kissing one's sister (if you are a male) or kissing your brother (if you are a female). It is nice but it does not stimulate. You have to know if you are winning or losing. Keeping score keeps the individual focused, gives instant feedback and provides a sense of family.

Work Should Be a Game: Since life is a series of games and since work occupies almost one-third of our life, it is safe to conclude that work is a game, perhaps not always fun, but nevertheless a game. Work is a game if there is a way to keep score. And, we know games are fun. Therefore, work should be fun. If not, then it is just plain labor, and not so much fun.

There are a lot of ways to keep score in the work place. For instance, safety records are scored by counting the days since the last lost time accident or the total number of people-hours worked safely since the last lost time accident. The score tells us that we have been victorious over accidents. These victories are duly noted by the addition of another safety jacket in the closet, another pizza for everyone on duty or some other form of company celebratory recognition. Production is scored daily or weekly with new records duly noted and highlighted. The annual report of the company dutifully reports the chairman's letter to the shareholders, the operating and manufacturing highlights of the year as well as the financial and statistical highlights. This is compared to previous years numbers thus providing a scorecard for the year's performance. Corporate America has a long history of providing a score for those things management believe to be "safe" or for the information they believe the employees should see.

Score Performance: The score should cover essentially all operating information, especially when operating in a *crisis transformation* mode. A company in a transformation situation should post the monthly financial statistics on the bulletin boards and comparc the essential control parameters to the results for last month, last year and to plan. Appropriate comments should accompany the scoreboard, that is, an outstanding performance should be noted and praised. A lesser performance should draw appropriate comment with suggestions of what is required to get back on plan. The safety scoreboard should record the safe hours and safe days. This can indicate if one is winning or if one is losing.

Celebrate, Celebrate, Celebrate: However, you cannot quit there, you must supply the missing ingredient, celebrate notable accomplishments. Organizations need to celebrate. Don't keep quiet about those things the organization wants done, let the team members (followers) know that they are noticed and appreciated. Celebrate.

Reward Achievement: Keeping score just for the sake of keeping score is not satisfying. When one wins there must be an appropriate award to the winners of each of these important games that are important to the company. Safety can be rewarded by safety dinners for

employees and their spouses (or significant others).

Culture Can Be a Factor: One of the more creative rewards we have seen was devised by a manager of a ship repair yard that at the time of our first meeting was having a perfectly horrible safety record. The facility was averaging one lost time accident per week! That is right, an average of one per week. His corrective plan of action addressed all of the pertinent cultural issues. His plan was as follows: Beginning on Monday when the employee reported to work, a playing (poker) card was drawn, this was repeated on Tuesday, on Wednesday, and on Thursday. The drawn cards were attached to the front of their respective lockers. On Friday morning the fifth card was drawn and the best "show down" poker hand got the day off with pay if there had been no lost time accident that week. The lost time accidents plummeted from an average of one a week to zero for the next 24 month period. To add to this incredible performance, the absenteeism was reduced to almost zero because you can't play the game if you aren't present to draw all five cards. An added benefit! The human result of this was that people were not being hurt and maimed.

The culture and the attitude of this operation changed remarkably. The attitude changed from everyone for himself to everyone looking out for everyone else. One could hear a worker call out to a fellow worker swinging out over the water with a large piece of plate steel, "Hey, be careful up there, I have a good poker hand going this week and I already have plans for my Friday off". It was said in jest but a real love and caring feeling developed over the months as the employees became aware that they could do a better job and they could also do it safely. A camaraderie developed.

The self-esteem soared and a justified pride became apparent. It was all mental. Think, think, and think. People thought about what had to be done, how it had to be done and thought about the worst downside risk of each task of each job and determined whether or not they could stand the downside risk before proceeding. It should be noted that the efficiency of this operation soared by over 20%. People cause accidents because they don't focus on the task and don't think the job through before acting. Mechanical failure causes only 2% of lost time accidents in industry. Keep score and see how it pays.

Miscellaneous Transformation Issues

Chapter 27

COACHING AND TEACHING

The obligation to coach: One of the very important obligations for the leader/manager is to provide continuous coaching and teaching for those with whom they work. Proper execution of this obligation is essential to the long-term health of the employees as well as to the long-term health of the corporate entity. Coaching and teaching can take many forms and can be done in a variety of ways depending upon the personality of the individuals involved. Coaching is not an obligation that is performed in a "sink or swim" environment. Again, this is completely dependent upon the personality of the "pupil" involved. The personality has to be evaluated constantly. It must be read and monitored as this process moves forward.

Don't Feed the Monkeys: The one critical mistake in this process which should not be committed by the manager is to take over a function or a project which has been delegated to the coached person, correct it or straighten it out, and then hand it back to him. This is tantamount to feeding the follower's monkey and this can lead to a manager running a large menagerie if they continue with this practice. The business of the manager is not to run a menagerie but to have solutions brought to her for discussion, for critique and for suggestions. This is the essence of coaching. The final execution of this must lie with the person being coached; otherwise learning does not take place. If empowerment has been usurped there is no growth in the individual.

Structure to Minimize Mistakes: For coaching to be effective one must have a pupil who is intelligent and is mentally and psychologically healthy. When assigning a task, the task must be challenging, the completion of the task must move the person up the learning curve. The goal must be clearly stated and the guidelines for obtaining that goal must be clearly delineated. Depending upon the personality, the method and technique for follow-up can be constant, periodic or at the completion of the task. This depends upon the relationship and the understanding between the individual and the coach. The critique of the completed project must be fair, must be equitable and it must clearly indicate where and how that the individual can improve next time. The appropriate recognition given to the individual depends upon their personality. The coach, knowing their psychological status will know how many strokes this individual should have and what kind or type of recognition is appropriate to fit the personality in order to provide the motivation to move further up the learning curve. Keep in mind that the ultimate goal of the coaching process is to produce a winning team and generally the team that makes the fewest number of mistakes is usually the one that wins.

The Meaning of Coaching: Coaches should be reminded that the ultimate trophy in this coaching effort is when they have coached a follower to the level that she can replace her. This is analogous to the goal of a good psychotherapist who helps her patient get to the point of being independent and able to function in life without psychotherapy. Only at the point when this capability exists is it possible for the individual to be promoted to a higher level of responsibility. Coaching at all levels (CEO, supervisor or technician) should be a part of the culture of the company. At the end of the day every employee should feel they have learned more than they knew at the beginning of the day and have expanded their knowledge base. Today we must be better than we were yesterday but not as good as we will be tomorrow.

Final Exams: The real test of the effectiveness of coaching is when the coach kicks the fledgling bird off the nest to see if it can fly. This is done when the person moves up to take over as the replacement for vacation relief or for some other caused absence. Or, the junior management has been coached and rehearsed on how to make effective presentations. The time to fly presents itself by an invitation from Senior Management to make a presentation to the Board of Directors and to stand up for "board type" questions from the board members. This permits the presenter to gain confidence in their ability to make presentations to a board and to deal effectively and spontaneously with the questions from the board members. This type of experience and exposure is very good training for the next level of promotion within the company. It can be very valuable if they were to move to a larger company. To have the confidence and the competence to effectively make presentations is a very important requirement for any position in a company. Persons with technical backgrounds, particularly engineers, are notoriously poor writers, speakers and listeners. They generally require more teaching and coaching in this area than do those schooled in liberal arts, legal, marketing and sales.

Miscellaneous Transformation Issues

Chapter 28

DECISION MAKING - ALWAYS TRUST YOUR GUT

Decisions and Stress: Decisions are very psychological in their making. The cause of much of our

stress is the requirement to make decisions. In fact decision-making can be so difficult for some people that they freeze up and cannot function when it becomes decision time. Decisions are never made before the time they absolutely have to be made. Whoever heard of a preemptive decision? Have you ever heard anyone say,"Sure, I think I will make this decision two weeks early so I will have more time later for non-decisions."

The Deadline is Never the Deadline: Decisions are made only against deadlines, and are made frequently after the deadline. One finds in the strategy of negotiation that the deadline is never the deadline. The real pearls of the negotiation fall out only at the deadline time. Decisions are much the same way. The trade-off gems that determine the final result usually fall out at the deadline, the time the juices are really flowing at their maximum.

The making of decisions is stressful, in fact, very stressful. This is the reason why one of the outstanding required personality characteristics of a good leader manager must be the ability to manage stress. This process can stimulate a good manager to a high level of excitement and performance. The adrenaline really flows. The adrenaline addicted manager must be watched and managed carefully as this is also found in the *crisis transformation* manager who will create a crisis in order have decisions to make in order for the adrenaline to flow. Beware of the addicted manager! You have previously been admonished to watch the *crisis transformation* manager.

The Misplaced Personality: Just as damaging to the organization as the addicted manager is the manager who cannot manage the stress associated with making decisions. This manager will defer the decision hoping the need will go away, or someone else will make it. When one cannot properly manage stress all sorts of psychological things begin to happen to the body. These include high blood pressure, acid stomach, etc. Stress causes illness. Stress can kill.

How Much Information is Enough: The primary thing that generates the stress level in most decision makers is the fact that seldom does one have all the information one would like to make the decision. Ideally, one would like to have the total facts and complete information relative to the subject so these could be a part of the computer's database. Who questions the computer's answer? However, if the facts and comprehensive calculations clearly delineate the obvious answer, then no decision is involved. This is the difference between an answer and a decision. In an answer, no gut is involved, no juices flow, no arteries constrict, the body does not go on red alert and the gut does not wrench. The problem arises when information is lacking or is incomplete. This void cannot be remedied before the deadline. When the time for the decision comes, the manager who can manage stress, will consider and analyze the information available at that "five minutes in time" and will make the best decision available with this information in order to adhere to the deadline. And most importantly he will not look back on that decision.

Don't Look Back: Great decision-makers understand one very vital thing. Decisions are time driven. The more time one has to wait before making the decision, the more information will be available. Consequently, one should not waste one's time by looking back at a later date when additional data are available. Admittedly, this could have led to a different decision. That does not make the initial decision wrong nor does it make the reconsidered one

correct. Rather, it only makes it different. The best decisions based upon all the pertinent facts at the time of the deadline are the correct decisions. So don't look back, unless one would like to run the risk of lessening one's self-confidence in the process.

The Decision-Maker Vs. The Data-Collector: We should not pass this issue of confidence without comment. This is critical also. One must be comfortable with one's capability such that they honestly believe that under the circumstances, with the information that was available, the very best decision was made. This confidence level is essential. It is just as essential not knowingly to do anything that would lessen or damage that confidence. Self-confidence can be fragile. Make a couple of bad decisions in a row and you will find a little voice saying all sorts of things to you like "Why don't we wait for more information on this one". So don't look back on the process unless you wish to run the risk of becoming a perpetual data collector instead of a decision-maker.

Trust Your Gut: It Knows a Lot: An integral but subjective part of decision making is that one must trust your gut. Don't make the decision until the gut feels right. Company "A" was considering a recovery process being offered by two companies. One was from a raw material supplier and the other a competing non-raw material company. The calculation presented to management by the planning group made the decision look easy. The numbers were clearly in favor of the non-raw material supplier.

It was so clear and obvious that the gut just could not get comfortable with the answer. Some answers look too easy, too pat. We labored over the numbers, the

assumptions and the scenario until we were well past the decision deadline. Still uncomfortable and unwilling to make a decision, which would commit the company for twenty years for the sizable project, we called a knowledgeable friend. The friend, who was very familiar with the technical and operational workings of the raw material supplier, was invited to walk around a lake and talk about the variables in this proposal. Out of this discussion came an alarming and critical fact, which had been overlooked. The recovered element in the raw material could vary by a factor of three, and further could be varied more if the raw material supplier chose to do so. The assumptions had been wrongly assumed to be uniform. Assumptions can influence the final conclusion more than any other piece of the process. Further, the preexisting long-term raw material contract had no provision to compensate for such variations. Needless to say, this altered the economics, and showed that the initial calculations had not arrived at the correct answer. Bad assumptions yield bad answers. This made the gut comfortable and the decision easy.

Personality

Chapter 29

JOB PERFORMANCE AND PERSONALITY

Personality Maintenance vs. Management Efficiency: Personality behavior patterns of the employee can create work problems. These behavior patterns are not to be thought of as a psychiatric or psychological illness requiring treatment. Rather, they are variations in normal

psychological life which are not disabilities preventing them from working successfully. However, unless they are managed and understood by their supervisor, they can create a problem in productivity through loss of effectiveness and efficiency.

Rule of Thumb: The following rule of thumb is useful in evaluating whether there is a negative business effect related to the employee's personality. If you are spending 25% more time supervising one person because of their personality than you are spending on average for the others, then you should make sure that you are getting at least 25% more output from that person. Otherwise, the higher than average maintenance required for the personality of this one person is making the supervisor's efforts inefficient and stealing managing time from the balance of the organization. The negative fallout from this arrangement reflects personality problems in the employee, the supervisor or perhaps both. This same general rule of thumb is applicable to other interactions such as between the CEO and the Corporate Board of Directors.

Personality Problems that Interfere with Work: In the material, which follows, we will discuss and provide examples of some of the more common kinds of personality problems, which may interfere with work. While these examples are maladaptive in terms of work, they still fall within the range of human behavior, which are not considered evidence of psychiatric disturbances.

THE PERSON WHO CAN'T QUITE FINISH A JOB OR SUBTLY CREATES PROBLEMS FOR OTHERS

One pattern that is destructive to job performance is the person who just can't quite finish a job. This person instead of openly refusing to do what is assigned, does things, which interfere with an ongoing activity or process. For example, instead of producing the standard number of units in a standard amount of time the person produces 10% fewer. While not enough to get the person fired, this behavior is enough to derail the production schedule. Such behavior is not enough to call attention on the part of the supervisor to the person that is openly defying. Nevertheless, at the end of the workday somehow the work just simply doesn't get done. This is temporarily a safe way of not cooperating and complying since it is covert and not easily recognizable. Often others are blamed for the shortfall. For example, one can always blame the equipment, the work situation, management, the weather, or assorted other things without calling attention to the fact that it is really the person and the person's personality that is interfering with the work situation.

The Person Who Behaves in Childish and Immature Ways

Another pattern that is destructive to job performance is found in the person who is childish. The essential feature is that the person has childish needs that have to be constantly met. As a result they are always bugging the supervisor or someone to do this or that for them. This personality can never be satisfied in terms of what they have, much like a young child can never be satisfied. For such an individual, no matter how much she is given, they will still continue to demand more. This kind of irritating behavior can obviously manifest itself in irrational demands. At the very least it causes co-workers to be upset and angry because people simply can tolerate childishness only so long in a work situation and especially when it is coming from an adult. If it is coming from a child and especially your own child you can tolerate it a while but even in this idyllic circumstance it also has its limits. A reasonable person ends up getting angry or expressing feelings in inappropriate actions or behaviors. Infantile and immature behavior on the part of an individual can require additional personality maintenance time by the supervisor.

A PERSON WHO IS CHRONICALLY TIRED AND SAD

A third pattern that interferes with job performance is found in someone who is chronically tired and sad. This assumes this state is not a function of some medical condition or a situation where there has been a recent death of a loved one. This state slows down an individual's capacity to associate and think. Physical movements are slowed making them more prone to accidents. They may become preoccupied with their own life or excessively worry about their family. All of these factors impair the person's productivity and capacity to work. If these features are present over an extended period they suggest a departure from a normal psychological state and warrant referral to your organization's EAP or their personal physician.

A PERSON WHO CAN'T TELL THE DIFFERENCE BETWEEN FACT AND FICTION

A fourth pattern of psychological functioning harmful to job performance is a disturbance in a person's ability to assess reality. By this we mean the ability of the person to know the difference between their inner feelings and perceptions and what is actually transpiring in their work situation. Not being able to separate out these two parts of a person's reality can lead to serious distortions. Whenever a person is having trouble in this area they customarily resort to the use of some sort of coping behavior as a way of trying to make sense. Some of the more common approaches are to deny that what others see as happening is really occurring or to put the blame on persons in their environment for problems which are really their own. The destructive potential for job performance of such an attitude is clear.

A PERSON WHO PAYS TOO MUCH ATTENTION TO DETAILS

A fifth pattern of psychological functioning harmful to job performance is found in the person who constantly micromanages. Although it is necessary for a manager to know the broad details of a company's functioning, needing to know every detail becomes a personality dysfunction. If a person is micromanaging they have insufficient time to think about an organization's future. The important question becomes why the manager behaves in this way. The basic reason has to be control. Either the person feels so megalomanic that they think the world cannot function without their supervision or they feel so insecure they micromanage to ensure others do not see their failings. Both reasons are maladaptive to not only the person but to the organization. Such persons need referral to an outside source to help them assume a more moderate approach to details. The CEO or supervisor needs to be alert to the reality of each individual's situation in order to deal judiciously with this type of employee.

A Person Who Lets Martial Problems Affect Work

A final personality pattern that is destructive to job performance is found in the person whose marriage is in the process of collapsing or where there has been a recent divorce.

Most executives, supervisors, technicians or other employees are married. Sometimes there is a feeling among the spouses of these individuals that their work is more important than their marriage. Good marital and family interactions are important, not only for the happiness of the individuals involved but also for successful performance at work. For this reason it becomes of major importance that from the CEO to the lowest paid employee, attention should be paid to personal significant relationships.

When a person marries, the mutual physical attraction and pleasure they receive from having someone else seemingly invest their whole being in their happiness often blind them. What both parties overlook at that particular moment, is the fact that each of the parties early emotional life will have a major determining impact on their marital happiness. For we all are essentially psychological prisoners of our past. We all carry baggage. Unless we go through a period of psychological treatment it is quite probable as the marriage unfolds that each of the spouses will repeat what happened to them in their own early childhood. They will also use the model of their own parent's interaction as a way of relating to their spouse once the early bloom has worn off in their marriage. These same features have a high potential for being thrust into work relationships.

Thus, for example, a man whose father spent a good deal of time away from the home is likely to have a greater likelihood of repeating this same pattern in his own marriage. The resulting loneliness experienced by his spouse can lead to all sorts of personal unhappiness as well as marital distress. This same person may be receiving more gratification from work than he or she does from their spouse and seemingly become "married" to their job.

When this happens one has to step back and try to understand why more gratification is coming from their work than from their interpersonal experience with their spouse. Sometimes if there has been some marital infidelity in their own parent's life or there is some continuing unhappiness in their marriage the individual may act out this unhappiness by entering into affairs in the work place. While this form of behavior is under more scrutiny today because of the laws surrounding sexual harassment it nonetheless continues to occur and is unlikely to ever vanish. The potential impact on productivity of the above behavior needs little discussion.

We believe that the individual who is working, as well as the individual who is staying home, needs to carefully monitor and evaluate their feelings about work versus feelings about their home life. Clearly some sort of balance must occur. If there is a disproportionate amount of time spent at work or a disproportionate amount of distress being expressed by one of the spouses then some careful independent assessment needs to be made of what is happening. Consulting with someone who is not involved in the situation will offer some significant benefits. There are numerous consultants to business and industry who focus on this issue.

The organization that demands loyalty to the corporation over loyalty to the family is in danger of creating problems for both parties. It is a form of harassment by the corporation and self-destructive behavior by the individual who agrees to put work over family. There is plenty of angst out there over the work-life balance. Sadly, many organizations do not consider this is short sighted and in the long run not really conducive to corporate success and stability of their own work force.

When a problem arises it is best for both of the spouses involved to seek consultation and guidance. Sometimes helping both the parties see the maladaptive roles that they are playing out at home and/or work can easily solve any problem. Such consultations are not consultations to label one or the other of the individuals involved as having some psychiatric illness. Rather these consultations are ones which are designed to help both parties see the various strengths and weaknesses which they individually possess and how these interact in terms of the stress they are feeling as a result of the conflict between work and home. At that point, they are often able to take corrective action. Such action may be simply clarifying their feelings and talking to their spouse or it may involve a referral to an appropriate counselor.

Manage the Personality-Not the Person

One of the best articles we have read dealing with work and marriage is noted below. It would apply to all levels of employment even though the title suggests it be solely for executives.

Fitzpatrick, John J. and Frances, Anne, (1986). Executives and their marriages, understanding growth and change. *New Jersey Bell Journal*, 32-41.

Personality

Chapter 30

REALITY TESTING

What is Reality Testing? We have found that one of the most important abilities in successful managers is good reality testing. It is important for the manager to understand

what is meant by our use of this term. Good reality testing is accurately matching external events with one's own internal perceptions. For example, if someone expresses anger in your presence it is not necessarily true that they are angry with you. Instead, they may be angry with other persons or issues and you are a convenient outlet for their feelings. If the CEO or management reacts as if a person's anger is something caused by them, they have the potential for responding in destructive ways. There are numerous features of reality testing which deserve comment. But before we do this, it is important to know something about the development of reality testing.

The Genesis of Reality Testing: Reality testing is something that literally begins quite early in life. At the time of birth, the child moves from the reality of being protected inside the mother's womb to the reality of the harsh physical world with the changes of temperature, demands to be fed, demands to be kept warm, etc. Thus, there is an initial rush of reality with which the infant has to cope. All of the five senses play a role in the subsequent development of ability to correctly assess reality. The reality of one's life constantly changes as you grow. The more demands that are placed on you the more opportunities that you have. If the person is for some reason not able to keep contact with reality then their world becomes increasingly distorted. It doesn't really matter how smart you are or how intelligent you are if you are unable to distinguish reality. You have a problem that cannot be overcome by brilliance, or intellect, or by cognitive training. Thus, reality testing is a very primitive early kind of developmental function that begins at birth and continues on throughout life.

DIFFERENT WAYS OF HANDLING REALITY

Denial: For example, people can pretend as if what is happening to them isn't really happening. In psychological parlance this mode of responding is called denial. Denial can be useful in life. For example, pain may be better tolerated by the use of denial. On the other hand, it can be maladaptive in a person who has terminal cancer who denies their impending death. By use of this defense they lose the opportunity to make final arrangements in terms of their personal financial affairs and deal with their feelings and relationships with their friends and relatives. This is the type of defense that is most likely present in persons who seem to never "hear" instruction given by their supervisor. This turning off of environmental stimili leads to mistakes and missed opportunities in the workplace. Each of the five senses can be involved in this distortion of reality.

Blaming others: Another way of dealing with reality is to act as if someone out in your environment is causing the problem rather than you. For example, you are angry about something but instead of recognizing that you are the cause, you accuse others of being angry. This problem can create significant difficulties because people don't like to be accused of wrong doings when they are innocent. Each of the five senses can be involved in this distortion of reality.

Body Aches and Pains: Another way which people have of dealing with reality is by translating their fears and concerns into bodily aches and pains. As long as you are concerned about an aching muscle or some other physical sensation you can pretend as if the emotions or feelings embodied in the aches and pains are not real. Many people who go to physicians, for example, with aches and pains are in reality translating their emotional concerns into physical complaints. Stress in the workplace can stimulate use of this way of dealing with reality in many persons. The result is missed days at work and decreased output. While tactile sensation may be more likely involved in the reality distortion, the other four senses may play a part.

Thinking Without Allowing for Variations in Meaning: Some people also deal with reality by insisting that what happens cannot have any nuances or variations of meaning. That is, ideas or situations are seen as black or white with no shades of gray. Thus, they immediately restrict themselves in appreciating life experiences. Based on our personal experience we believe this kind of thinking is present in approximately 80% of the population regardless of their sex, age, race, social, educational or ethnic background. While this way of coping with reality can be managed by a high level of structure it becomes a real handicap for employees above the level of Technicians.

An example of how this kind of thought process affects daily living can be illustrated by the accepted political axiom that in a Presidential campaign 80% of the people have already decided how they will vote. The politicians then contest the remaining 20%. Since we know that at best only 50% of eligible voters go to the polls, it becomes possible that major elections are decided by only 10% of our population. Thinking in absolutes is one of the reasons negative campaign ads and promises made but never kept by politicians is so effective. No wonder the "spin doctors" appear so effective.

Advertising executives make use of the fact that a large percentage of persons have this kind of reality testing. There is no-in-between-statements made about such products as mouthwash, toothpaste, etc. The consumer is not advised that some variation in their usefulness might occur, or, that one product might be more useful to one person rather than the next. Rather, the statements are pitched to those 4 out of 5 people in the general population who are uncritical in evaluating statements. Some recognition of this problem is evident in the mild disclaimers noted in recent advertising of prescription drugs.

Helping You Manage: The foregoing are some of the main mechanisms that people use for dealing with reality. They are not all of the mechanisms used but they are probably the more frequent and more common ways that people have of dealing with reality. While occasional use of these mechanisms may not always handicap a person in a major way, their repeated use will. The reason for this extensive discussion of reality testing is that the manager needs to be aware that not only are these mechanisms operative in him or herself but they are also operative in their superior and those they supervise. They are most decidedly operative in the customers and other constituencies of the company. Knowing that these mechanisms are ever present should be a basis for helping them manage not only their interpersonal relationships with their colleagues, but, also should be a basis for helping them manage sales to customers, plan marketing strategies and produce better strategic plans.

Personality

Chapter 31

PERSONALITY WINS OVER SKILLS

The reader will recall our position that successful management must assume that an individual's performance

on a job is determined more by their personality and emotional state than by their skills. We hope that some of the positions we have taken will generate thought and discussion among those who read this contribution. We have no problem with those who disagree.

The Odds in Picking Personnel

The Best Odds: It is our position that the custom fitting of an individual's personality to the group with whom they work is a most critical issue at all levels within an organization. This custom fitting can be accomplished by specific individual matching or by a management that understands how to deal with individual variations in personality. It is very important certainly at the technician level. At this level, the organization wishes the task to be done the same way every time. No experimentation and no innovation are allowed at this level without the benefit of prior testing, analysis, and documentation. Documentation is required before any change becomes part of the standard operating procedure. Structure is the main ingredient of the job. It is our impression that four out of five people within the general population requires structure and avoidance of ambiguity. Therefore, since most of the technicians will be drawn from that 80% of the population, then fitting the personality to that requirement should, by pure statistics and demographics, become a much simpler task. You have four chances in five of choosing a person who requires structure. Custom fitting the personality to the supervisor, manager, and the leader positions becomes a little more challenging. One obvious reason for that is that the numbers and the odds begin to work against you.

How to increase the odds for success: To demonstrate what happens to the odds whenever you make skills paramount, let us consider the ideal population from which to pick the supervisor or manager. Remember our earlier discussion that employees in this category fall in the 20% of the population that has the capability to deal with ambiguity. The ability to deal with ambiguity is critical to being a good manager or being a good supervisor. If you are picking from the general population, you have one chance in five, of finding someone who can deal with ambiguity. Then, if you make the skill requirement paramount in the selection you have reduced the odds significantly. For example, if the technical skills you require are found only one time in 500 when added to the one in five personality match you have now increased the odds to one chance in 2,500 of finding the person who has the personality fit and the requisite technical job skills. This is only for the first line supervision! If we move up one more level, additional management skills are required. However, we are now picking from the previously screened first line of supervisors, so the odds of finding someone with the requisite technical skills should be lessened to say, one in ten. This increases the odds to 1 in 25,000! And, if we move one more level up the organization to middle management, then we leap to one in 250,000! We are still dealing with the one in five who can deal with ambiguity but now we have just jacked this number up from one in 25,000 to a number that becomes very, very large. There should be little wonder that we see so many misplaced people in management. So, one practical way to deal with this is to critically analyze whether there is an absolute need for the technical skills or whether the requisite technical skills can be taught on a reasonable basis in terms of costs and time, thus permitting an emphasis on the required management skills and personality. Make sure the individual has the personality that can deal with ambiguity because the management skills are transferable, and technical skills can be taught.

SOME CURRENT APPROACHES TO ASSESSMENT

Assessment of the personality of individuals can be a highly controversial issue. This is especially true, given EEOC requirements and the recent Americans with Disabilities Act. However, within the past few years there has been a resurgence in interest in assessing personality as it relates to success in business and industry. The interested manager can always avail themselves of professional help from a specialty group among psychologists involved in consulting to business and industry. Further information can be obtained from the American Psychological Association in Washington, D.C.

The Americans With Disability Act has complicated decisions as to whether testing is permissible at a pre-employment level. For example, psychological tests, which can be considered as medical (e.g. leading to a psychiatric diagnosis), cannot be given at a pre-employment level. They can be given at a post-employment level as long as all employees are included. However, if tests measure normal personality, it is generally agreed they do not fall under the purview of the Americans with Disability Act and therefore can be given.

Many of the better-known tests depend on the individual being able to read and record a response to the questions that are asked. One objection to tests such as the MMPI or MMPI-2 is that the content of the questions asked are considered as being invasive of an individual's privacy. Norms by which these tests are interpreted are gained by testing large groups of people. The groups are made up of samples, which statistically reflect such variables as age, sex, race, education level, and nationality. They may require up to an hour and a half on the part of each individual for completion. There is, in addition, time required by the consulting psychologist to complete the analysis of the test responses and prepare a report. Even if the constraints imposed by the ADA were not an issue, these requirements make it quite costly in terms of the selection process. This is true both in terms of time spent on the part of the applicant and the organization that has to defer making decisions based on the time needed to analyze and complete the testing.

Psychological tests are preferable to an interview on the part of the manager or peers in a given department simply because there is no way of controlling the impact of the personality on the interview of the manager or prospective co-workers. Then add the fact that most managers or Human Relations Departments simply do not have the skills or training to assess personalities accurately and one has a compelling argument for using appropriate assessments of personality.

We have noticed that if persons in a particular department are involved in interviewing and selecting their replacements or a new colleague, an interesting phenomenon occurs. The personality of the person they select most often is similar to them. Of course, this is helpful if the individuals doing the selection have the type of personality that functions well in the work setting. The downside comes when a given department is dysfunctional. Persons chosen by the individuals in such a department are more likely to have dysfunctional personality traits. The net result is that the efficiency and the effectiveness of the department cannot improve.

A DIFFERENT APPROACH

A newer and different approach to study of

personality is called the (RAP) Rousey Assessment of Personality. This test utilizes an approach wherein speech and hearing patterns of the person are assessed and related to normal psychological growth and development. The speech and hearing patterns that are analyzed do not fit the behavior that would qualify as a disability under Social Security regulations. Further, these patterns are not listed in the official Diagnostic and Statistical Manual used by psychiatrists or psychologists as necessary or required in making psychiatric diagnoses. Of further importance is the fact that racial or linguistic backgrounds are taken into account in the study of speech and hearing patterns.

This assessment can be administered within five minutes as opposed to the longer time required for administration of many more well known psychological tests. One of the virtues of this particular approach is that one is able to standardize norms for each organization and company on a local basis with a minimum of time involved. Since this standardization can be related statistically to criterion related parameters, it offers acceptable standards for validation using EEOC criteria. Thus, regional norms or local norms rather than national norms are available.

This approach is based on research studies completed at the Minnesinger Clinic that began in the mid-to-late 1960s. The Menninger Clinic is an internationally known psychiatric treatment center who pioneered the application of psychological principles to the needs of individuals in business and industry. By focusing on a person's speech and hearing patterns, the test is non-threatening. It doesn't invade their privacy in the sense of asking them if they hate their mother or if they engage in unusual sexual activities, etc. Finally, the norms for each organization can be constantly updated because of the brevity of time of administration and the fact that the test itself can be computerized and norms established in that fashion. We have found this especially important since all organizations have their own personalities.

Assess the personality of all employees: Tests, despite any of their shortcomings, are preferable to interviews simply because it is impossible to standardize interviews or to develop norms. The authors obviously hold a strong bias towards the need to test all potential employees for all positions. This is even more important in transformation situations. An assessment of the personality is critical to placing the employee and matching that employee with the individuals with whom they work. We previously talked about testing for the technical capabilities but again if there is any doubt between personality and technical capabilities always go with the personality. While the cost of dealing with an under qualified employee can be significant, the technical side can be taught in a reasonable period of time and at a predetermined cost. However, the cost of a misfit on the psychological side can have a very significant impact along with undeterminable costs beyond the single position this employee may occupy.

Fit the personality to the job and to the group: In the case of a mature organization, it is helpful to determine the personality profile of the overall organization and of the various departments within it. This will permit the best placement of new employees who may be entering this particular work force. An example of this is the case of a company, which had a sales force of ten people including the head of sales. The individuals of the sales force had been tested to determine those personality traits, which were deemed critical to the required performance of a sales representative. When interviewing for a replacement, a number of attractive candidates were interviewed and ultimately five of these were tested to determine where the strongest points of correlation of the personality profile were with the common characteristics, which the previous testing of the sales group had revealed. True, first impressions are lasting impressions, although, not always correct. The interview process has become so highly tutored, practiced and refined by use of video playback, coaching, role model, etc., that you cannot be sure you are "seeing" the real person during the interview process. It should be added that you cannot always rely on references. Convinced that some of the interviewees had been highly coached in the techniques of interviewing, this possibility was taken into consideration as the person chosen based upon the RAP did not interview as well as the other candidates. However, in actual practice this individual moved effortlessly into the sales clan and became a high level producer with a high level of reality testing thus validating the decision to look beyond the process to the personality.

Understanding the personality assures better management: The testing of present employees, even though they may be long-term successful employees, can be of great interest in establishing a baseline for the normal personality which functions most effectively in that organization. The concept of success needs to be defined carefully to EEOC standards or criterion related validity. Having such norms can be of great assistance in evaluating one's performance or particularly, the lack of one's performance. An example of this is the case where a newly hired (and highly recommended by her former employer and the headhunter) department head failed to perform to the competent level. The issue seemed to be this person's inability to stay focused on any particular subject or particular issue. She kept taking mental excursions in the middle of a discussion.

The personality evaluation test revealed that this person did indeed have difficulty of focusing for more than very brief periods and subsequent referral for a medical examination found there was a physiological reason for the difficulty. This is an example of how understanding what is a normal personality for an organization can result in an appropriate referral to ensure a healthy and productive employee. Understanding the personality of current employees can alert management to being more supportive and encouraging than otherwise might be the case. For example, one employee revealed during testing the need for more than the usual amount of praise and support. Management was then able to help the person succeed by use of judicious positive verbal feedback and recognition.

Suggested Reading

Following are some additional reading sources for other approaches:

Hogan, R., Hogan, J., & Roberts, B. (1996). Personality measurement and employment decisions. *American Psychologist, 51*, 469-477.

Holland, J. (1996). Exploring careers with a typology. *American Psychologist, 51,* 397-406.

Inwald, R., & Reko, J. (1995). Preemployment screening for public safety personnel. In: *Innovations in Clinical Practice: A Source Book, Vol. 14,* 363-380.

Levinson, H. (1990). Criteria for choosing chief executives, *Harvard Business Review, 2,* 113-120.

Rousey, C., Morrison, D., & Deacon, D. (1995). Choosing successful management. *Consulting Psychology Journal, 47*, 108-113.

Tett, R., Jackson, D., & Rothstein, M. (1991). Personality measures as predictors of job performance: A meta-analytic review. *Personnel Psychology, 44,* 703-742.

APPENDIX

UNDERSTANDING EXECUTIVES BY USE OF SPEECH AND HEARING *

The failure rate and/or managerial incompetence among executives is estimated to range from 50-75% (Hogan, et.al, 1988 and DeVries, 1992 as cited in: Hogan et al, 1994). Therefore, the economic and human need for procedures to help understand what makes a successful executive is obvious. How could it be that a 5 to 10 minute structured sample of a person's speech and hearing behavior would be useful in defining successful and unsuccessful executives? In answering this question we will present:

First - past approaches and rationales for study of an executive's personality;

Second - basic information about speech and hearing;

- Adaptation of Paper Presented August 17, 1997 to American Psychological Association Meeting in Chicago, Illinois

Third - a theory, which relates speech and hearing to normal personality;

Fourth - the results of applying this theory to various levels of personnel and executives, and

Fifth - potential applications of this theory in business and industry.

PAST APPROACHES

A representative discussion of methods for study of executive performance can be found in Levinson, 1980; Clark and Clark, 1988; Baehr, 1992 and Jaques and Cason, 1994. Within the past few years there has been increasing data and support for the assessment of personality as a predictor of job performance and executive success. Recent publications in this regard include the works of Tett, et al 1991, Levinson, 1994 and Hogan, et al, 1996. What is common to all of the above approaches is their dependence on the use of spoken and written language. One of the problems in the use of any form of language is the multiple meanings of words themselves as well as the over determination involved in an individual's reactions to these words.

BASIC INFORMATION REGARDING SPEECH AND HEARING BEHAVIOR

Psychologists are accustomed to using the terms, *speech* and *language,* interchangeably. In this discussion, it is important to make a distinction. As used in this paper, the term ***language*** will refer to the various symbolic concepts that become attached to various combinations of sounds or written characters. In contrast, use of the term ***speech*** will refer to individual sounds, which can occur both within and without the context of spoken language.

The production of speech (i.e., sounds) used in spoken language is customarily understood in academic circles, such as linguistics or speech pathology, by use of various cognitive or neurogenic constructs (Stoel-Gammon, 1985; Shriberg, et al, 1997). This paper will focus on an alternative understanding of speech and hearing behavior, which can help us understand the variations, which occur in an executive's personality.

The many variables, which can be identified in speech and hearing behavior, allow for a complex formulation of psychological life. For example, there are at least 26 vowel sounds in General American, Eastern and

Southern speech. Twenty-five consonants (many appearing at the beginning, middle and end of words) are easily heard. Production of the consonants and vowels may be further delineated by noting whether, they are accurate, distorted, omitted or one sound is substituted for another. There is clinical experience to expect that in the absence of psychological stress, a person can make from 12-14 different tone steps from their lowest to highest tone. At least 20 different adjectives can be used in describing a person's voice quality. Study of swallowing patterns suggests at least two basic kinds. During testing of the localization of sound, six tones ranging from 250 Hz to 4000 Hz are used with at least 23 possible responses available. Since all of the above data have discrete psychological meanings alone and different meanings in interaction with one another, it is easy for a person adept at permutations and combinations to estimate the potential complexity of personality, which can be generated by study of these variables.

Before going further in the exposition of the theory relating speech sounds and psychological development it is useful to address the issue of how much a person's anatomy and neurological integrity affect speech production. From both clinical observation and controlled experiments we know that the lips, tongue, teeth and breathing play at most a minor role in the ability to make sounds. That is, removal of the tongue secondary to cancer or the presence of cleft palate or lip does not preclude the correct production of the sounds used in speech. We also know that even in a profoundly deaf child, the speech sounds common to the infant 6 months of age and younger are made without problems and that short of a profound hearing loss, speech production is not significantly impaired.

Studies of the use of specific consonant sounds show there is no universal pattern of consonant acquisition past the first year (Templin, 1957). Further, McDonald (1964) has demonstrated that even in cases where consonant production difficulty is present, it is always possible to demonstrate that this is not a consistent phenomenon. This is in contrast to the nearly universal mastery of all vowel sounds by the first six months of life and the rare problem in vowel production after that period.

SPEECH PRODUCTION and NORMAL PSYCHOLOGICAL DEVELOPMENT

There are some striking similarities between speech and hearing development and the psychological birth and growth of a person as conceptualized in psychoanalysis (Rousey, 1997). Sounds used in spoken language are either vowels or consonants. **Vowels** may be defined as sounds produced without any stoppage of airflow such as might be occasioned by lip closure or movement of the tongue. In contrast, **consonants** may be defined as sounds produced by stoppage of air and sound by contact with any of the various speech articulators such as the lips, teeth and hard or soft palate.

During the first year of a child's life there appears all of the individual sounds, which will be later used to make up spoken language (Irwin, 1947; Irwin 1948). The majority of sounds, which are present in the first six months of a child's life, are vowels while the majority of sounds, which make their appearance in the last six months of the first year of life, are consonants.

We postulate that the concurrent development of vowels and drives in the infant and the beginning development of object relationships coincident with the appearance of consonants, while not causal are connected. The above possibility first came to awareness in 1965 when Rousey and Moriarty (1965) studied the speech and hearing behavior of a group of normal children whose early psychological life had been extensively documented by Lois Murphy (1962). Post-dictions about the connections between speech sounds and psychological development in these children were determined to be correct 83% of the time.

DRIVE EXPRESSION AS REFLECTED IN VOWELS

It is a common observation that an infant in the first few months of life express their feelings of discomfort, hunger or pleasure by the production of sounds, which when phonetically studied are principally vowels. It is a further common observation that sounds of displeasure made by adults at an athletic contest are not long reasoned discourses made up of words but rather vowel like sounds of disgust or pleasure depending on the official's call. Similarly, the sounds made during sexual intercourse are generally vowels as opposed to consonants. It is also an assumption in psychoanalytic theory that the main emotional life of the early infant is the expression of affect and drives. Since early drive expression in the infant is diffuse and only grossly structured and since the process of vowel production has little containment or structure we associate vowels with expression of drive.

The connection between vowels and drive expression can be illustrated by several everyday examples. For example, persons from England are considered more inhibited in drive expression (and have clipped vowels) while persons from Spanish cultures (have extended vowels) are considered as expressing their drives more freely. The main speech difference between Southern, Eastern and General American cultures found in the United States are, not surprisingly, found in vowel production. Thus, it is not too surprising that drive expression is slightly different in various regions of the United States. Correction of a foreign dialect speech pattern involves changing of vowels rather than consonants. This occurs quite easily in persons willing to adopt and adapt to the prevailing culture (i.e., drives) in which they find themselves.

OBJECT RELATIONSHIPS AS REFLECTED IN CONSONANTS

With reference to the position that consonants reflect object relationships, consider the fact that it is only with the appearance of consonants that vowels can be contained and organized to allow interpersonal relationships to occur. Illustrative of this assertion is that the earliest words made by most children (mama, dada) are a function of consonants shaping vowels which allow a child to relate to the two most important objects in their early life.

There are other everyday observations, which support the notion that consonant usage is related to interpersonal (object relationship development) functioning. For example, it is quite common for a person's speech intelligibility (which is a function of consonant production) to be impaired where a greater than average degree of anxiety is present. This was observed and demonstrated by Bradford (1961) when the speech patterns of female college freshmen were observed while reading a word list with an equal number of sexual and neutral words containing the sound "s". During this experiment a pronounced whistle was observed on the "s" sound in words such as penis, sex, as compared to words such as bus, sun. Whether a similar degree of anxiety with this paradigm would be present in today's culture is open to question. Slips of the tongue as noted by Freud principally involve consonants and always occur in interpersonal situations (Rousey, 1971).

It is possible to propose some association between personality development and consonant production if one examines the pattern of mastery of these sounds as reported by Templin (1957). Five clusters of consonants can be assembled if one assumes a cut-off point of 90% or greater as reflecting some degree of general mastery. In the theory being described in this appendix the various sounds in each cluster are assumed to reflect mastery of the five major stages of psychosexual development rather than only ability to make a sound.

The reasoning behind the assignment of sounds to psychosexual stages can be illustrated as follows. For example, the L sound (as in the word lady) is believed associated with the oral receptive stage. This assumption is made because cineradiographic studies of the production of the L sound demonstrate the same movements are also made during nursing. The R sound (as in the word run) is similar to the grunting sound made by the child during defecation and hence postulated as associated with the anal period. Finally, the th sound (as in words them or thanks) is made by the protrusion of the tongue between the teeth. Since analytic writers posit the tongue as having phallic meaning, the production of this sound is understood as a reflection of the phallic period.

VOICE QUALITY AND NORMAL PSYCHOLOGICAL DEVELOPMENT

Voiced sounds such as vowels can also be described in qualitative terms. While some consonant sounds require voicing, the majority of voiced sounds are vowels. It will be recalled that vowels are assumed to reflect drive states. The quality that one hears in voiced sounds is understood as a reflection of both internal and external factors. There are at least 20 different descriptive labels that can be applied to voice (e.g., breathy, hoarse, aphonic, etc.). Everyday examples of how voice quality reflects the psychological state of the individual illustrate the premise we are using. Every parent knows the psychological meaning of the infant who needs changing or the break in a child's voice about to cry or who has been caught with their hand in the proverbial cookie-jar. A similar kind of break in an adolescent male is normally associated with the onset of puberty and partially understandable in terms of the rapid growth of vocal chords. It can also be understood as symptomatic of the many fluctuating emotions, which are present at that age. Generally we feel comfortable in identifying masculinity and femininity by voice quality.

TONE VARIATIONS AND NORMAL PSYCHOLOGICAL DEVELOPMENT

The capacity to make discrete tone steps from the lowest to highest pitch involves use of vowels. Since vowels are assumed to reflect drives, it is postulated that the capacity to make different tone steps reflects the affect connected with the drives. A reduced capability is presumed to reflect affect inhibition. This can be illustrated by our pleasure with the tonal variations in our own voice while singing in the shower as compared with making the same sounds in a public situation.

Of sociological interest is that at least some American Indians, prior to aggressive forays, would engage in the practice of what they called toning. In a slightly different form the practice continues today by professional singers as they "warm up" before performing. Both of these latter examples are similar to what is here described as producing tonal variations from the highest to lowest note and understood as attempts to loosen up drive expression.

SWALLOWING AND NORMAL PSYCHOLOGICAL DEVELOPMENT

The next assumption made in the theory being described is that how a person swallows is related to psychological development. The usual way of swallowing is to retract one's tongue and throw the bolus of food down the esophagus. However, at birth, it is easy to observe that the tongue protrudes when swallowing. This same observation can be made in the normal development of children until around age 5 years when approximately 95% of children swallow in the manner described above. There has never been any data to support the premise that the shift in swallowing is related specifically to neurological or anatomical factors. In the present theory the position is taken that the disappearance of the tongue thrust around age five is related to the resolution of normal competitive feelings the child has in their relationship with their mother and father. In everyday life one has only to observe the tongue in pictures of athletes at the moment of achievement (e.g., Michael Jordan making a slam dunk) to make the association between tongue thrusting and competition. Another example of the association between competitiveness and tongue thrusting can be seen in children sticking out their tongue at each other during altercations.

SOUND LOCALIZATION AND NORMAL PSYCHOLOGICAL DEVELOPMENT

Because of the nature of the human auditory system, reality dictates that a simultaneously and binaurally presented pure tone should be reported as being perceived or localized somewhere either inside the head or at both ears. In a child below 3 years of age, when given the opportunity to localize the sound anywhere, one gets reports of the sound as coming from outside their person, in only one ear, parts of their body, etc. Observation also demonstrates that as the child grows older, there is increased awareness of the reality of the stimulus origin. The place of localization reflects the psychological defenses, which are being used. For example, localizing the tone in one ear when in reality it is in both ears is consistent with A. Freud's (1946) definition of denial.

CLINICAL STUDIES UTILIZING THE THEORY

One way to validate the forgoing theory presumed to describe normal psychological development, as reflected through speech and hearing behavior, is to observe such behavior in individuals with defined psychological disturbance. This approach is in keeping with what proponents of the Five Factor Model of Personality have done (Clark, et al, 1994). As a consequence of a NIMH Post-doctoral grant to the present author, it became possible to gather speech and hearing data on a large number of psychiatric patients. Over the course of 10 years, studies of specific clinical entities plus specific research projects were completed. How speech and hearing behavior varied in psychiatric patients was documented (Rousey, 1974a). Data generated by this theory was compared to data obtained by psychologists and psychiatrists. The population involved ranged from preschool to senior citizens. It is relevant to note that none of the psychiatric diagnoses used at that time or since have ever specified, used or been dependent on the assumptions of the present theory.

Two studies (Kernberg and Rousey, 1970; Fleming and Rousey, 1974) demonstrated that a speech and hearing evaluation made before and after the completion of psychotherapy reflected changes, which occurred as well as changes which did not. Ware and Rousey (1977) also noted similar findings in their study of psychological change in a therapeutic nursery school. Studies have been completed of how speech patterns reflect potential for destructive behavior to self or others (Mehrhof and Rousey, 1971) and how speech patterns are able to contribute to the prediction of violence in children (Filippi and Rousey,1971). Speech residues of early father-child disturbance were studied by LaFon and Rousey (1970). Unique speech patterns were identified in school underachievers (Sehdev and Rousey, 1974) and in childhood pseudo-mental retardation (Norris, 1974). Levy (1974) demonstrated how educators could use the theory.

Study of other groups such as orphans (Wells, 1972) and delinquents (Rousey & Averill, 1963 and Cozad & Rousey, 1966) also noted greater than predicted problems in speech production. McDowell, 1968 and Cantwell, et al, 1981 have also reported on the high incidence of speech problems in psychiatric patients.

Brende & Rinsley (1979) discussed variations in speech sounds, which occur in the phenomenon of persons speaking in tongues. Among a group of student nurses in a group sensitivity experience, use of the theory presently espoused was demonstrated as useful in understanding the group process (Fagundes, 1974).

APPLICATIONS OF THE THEORY WITH PERSONNEL & EXECUTIVES

Having seen that variations in speech and hearing occur in a known clinical population in a way predicted by the theory, the next step was to assess whether variations of speech and hearing behavior would have meaning in populations other than children or psychiatric patients.

A standard protocol was developed and has been used for the last twenty-five years for this effort. It was initially applied in work with executives and managers at the Center For Applied Behavioral Science at the Menninger Clinic and since has been used in various work settings. Five areas of speech and hearing behavior are studied during an approximate 5-10 minute interview.

Area One - The person is asked to read aloud a list of 50 words containing the most commonly used consonants and vowels in spoken language in the United States. The words used are easily read by someone with a 6th grade level of reading. If dyslexia or a mental age of 3 years are present the words can be repeated after the examiner.

Area Two - An observation and description of the person's voice quality is made during the reading of these words.

Area Three - An observation and description of the swallowing pattern is completed.

Area Four - The person is asked to make as many different tone steps as possible from the lowest to highest tone using the syllable *la*. Experience has shown that most people become confused if they are asked to sing the musical scales using *do, re, me,* etc.

Area Five - The person is asked to localize the source of a simultaneously and binaurally presented pure tone in different frequencies ranging from 250 Hz to 4000 Hz. They are given instructions similar to what is used in projective tests. That is, they are free to localize the sound as originating from anywhere.

PILOT STUDIES INVOLVING NORMAL INDIVIDUALS OTHER THAN EXECUTIVES

Prior to reporting how this technique was utilized with executives, it will be useful to review the results of some pilot studies, completed prior to 1974, of personnel selection and retention. In these studies only areas one and two were utilized.

In the first pilot study, (Rousey, 1970) investigated who would be selected for duty in the armed forces. The initial sample involved was small due to the level of cooperation we could obtain. Among 6 recruits (three independently declared successful and three declared failures by the armed services) we observed that success or failure was related to speech data which allowed inferences regarding ability to control impulses and get along with others. Using these parameters we were able to correctly identify acceptance or rejection in all six applicants.

Next we studied 18 armed forces personnel who were psychiatrically hospitalized. We assumed that, by definition, the fact that the 18 had to be hospitalized would be criteria for identifying them as having troubles in adjusting. Again using the above criteria we were able to identify 14 out of the 18 persons who were referred for hospitalization.

In study two (Rousey, 1972), eighty three applicants for a variety of job tasks at a large industrial complex were assessed on a serial basis to predict who would be hired and who would remain on the job after three months. Their speech was recorded by personnel of the industry participating in the study. Since these persons did not know the results of the speech analysis, it did not play a part in whether the individual was hired, terminated if hired or left the job for other reasons. The tape recordings were analyzed blindly and predictions made about job status solely on the basis of their speech behavior and rated as plus (meaning success) or minus meaning(failure). Of the 54 applicants rated as minus only 11 were employed after three months. Of the 29 applicants rated as plus 14 were employed after three months. Thus, roughly there was a one in five chance that successful employment occurred if there was some variation in speech as opposed to a one in two chance for successful employment if there was none. Study of the financial aspects of employees who were predicted to be unsuccessful but nonetheless hired and later quit or were terminated demonstrates that approximately four times more was paid than to employees rated as successful who later quit or were terminated.

In our third pilot study (Rousey, 1973) twenty office workers in a professional setting were studied to determine if longevity of employment could be predicted based on assessment of their psychological life through speech and hearing patterns. All five areas of the above protocol were utilized. Five of the group had been employed for over 24 months. In this group inferences made from the speech and hearing assessment demonstrated that there was a normal range of affect, no disturbance in reality testing and no early object relationship conflicts. In contrast in five employees who had been on the job between 12-18 months, three were terminated. Two of them had frank breaks in reality testing and one was in constant need of support and nurturance secondary to an early object relationship disturbance with their mother or mothering substitute. The two persons remaining employed had numerous somatic complaints. Ten persons were employed up to 11 months. However, 8 of these had been terminated. Of these 8, five exhibited disturbances in reality testing as reflected on their responses during the sound localization test. The other three individuals were in constant need of nurturance and support secondary to an early object relationship disturbance with their mother or mothering substitute.

With the experience gained in the foregoing experiments and the addition of data from all five areas, two predictive studies were completed to further test the validity of the theory. The first study involved applicants applying for a psychiatric residency program at Menninger (Rousey, 1974b). Nineteen individuals were involved. They were given the speech and hearing protocol during their initial visits for residency consideration. The findings regarding their speech and hearing behavior was written and placed under seal only to be opened three years later when a residency would have been completed were it started. At the end of the three-year period a comparison was made between the written speech predictions and the findings of the faculty of the residency training program. The two areas, which seemed to differentiate between successful residents versus those who were not accepted centered around capacity for object relationships and ability to express and experience affect. Using these two areas correct predictions were made in 14 of the 19 candidates. Three more of the candidates were predicted to be rejected or have problems by the speech protocol but accepted by the interview committee. All three of these individuals required psychological care during the course of their training. The remaining two candidates were endorsed by the speech protocol but rejected by the interview committee. These rejections occurred despite numerous positive comments in their interview records.

A second study (Rousey and Mitchell, 1974) involved application of the speech and hearing protocol to select 15 clergy involved in a pastoral care and counseling program. Eight were applicants and 7 were already in the program. Utilizing speech and hearing data, which reflect affect capability and capacity for reality testing, it was possible to predict acceptance or rejection accurately in 7 out of the 8 applicants. In the 7 persons already involved in training it was possible to identify accurately problems in affect, reality testing and expression of aggression. In all instances predictions were made independent of faculty evaluations or ongoing training records and kept under seal until the end of the training process.

For the next 20 years the use of the speech and hearing protocol was applied in our work with various organizational consultants. One group (Morrison Associates) utilized this assessment with over 650 executives. We (Rousey, Morrison and Deacon, 1995) studied the speech and hearing behavior of three groups of executives (successful, marginal and at risk for job loss). They were picked by Morrison on the basis of his individual consultations and work with the individual's organizations. There were 30 persons in each group.

Group l: (Successful) were composed of executives considered by colleagues as a leader, personally feeling successful and seen by peers, subordinates and superiors as successful.

Group 2: (marginally successful) were composed of persons who had serious psychological problems unknown to most people (e.g., alcoholism, family problems, etc.).

Group 3: (at risk for job loss) were composed of individuals with serious performance and interpersonal problems at work, were terminated or about to be terminated or had a serious mental illness including but not limited to drug addiction or high risk for suicide.

When the psychological implications of their speech and hearing behavior were translated, **Group one,** the successful group demonstrated good reality testing, only a moderate affect inhibition, were able to support and nurture the efforts of others and were hypercritical of their own performance.

Group two (the marginally successful) felt deprived in their early nurturing relationships with their mother or mother substitute, were at risk for alcohol or substance abuse, were not hypercritical of their own performance and were chronically inhibited.

In contrast, the persons in **Group three,** who were at risk for losing their jobs, 1), felt even more deprived in nurturing and supporting the efforts of others, 2), needed structure to integrate what was happening in their environment, 3), had impaired reality testing in situations where creativity was required and, 4), were inhibited in their affect life.

All three groups had a good ability to learn, good early relationships with their father or father substitute and had a good sense of sexual identity.

Chroniak (1996) replication of the above findings used the same population but with different subjects utilized 120 executives (60 categorized successful and 60 categorized unsuccessful.) Chroniak's definition of groups were essentially the same as reported earlier in the Rousey, Morrison and Deacon study. He did not have the advantage of having personally completed a consultation on each person, as was the case in the first study. Subjects were selected solely from reading the social history and applying the above criteria. Reliability studies using three psychologists demonstrated 100% agreement with the initial categorization made by Chroniak.

Computer generated descriptive statements of personality (Rousey and Rousey, 1995) related to specific speech and hearing data were available to describe the groups. Chroniak (1996) found successful executives in contrast to executives who were in trouble:

1 - were able to develop and maintain healthy interpersonal relationships

2 - were able to deal successfully with their aggressive impulses

3 - could integrate and synthesize ideas, feelings and emotions

4 - had defenses which were flexible and adaptive

5 - had appropriate ego boundaries

6 - had a good sense of identity

7 - had good reality testing.

His findings, while more specific due to the availability of computer generated statements about the meanings of speech and hearing variations essentially replicated the earlier conclusions of Rousey, Morrison and Deacon (1995). Further, they were in keeping with other investigator's descriptions of effective leaders (Zaleznik and de Vries, 1975; Kernberg, 1979; Levinson and Rosenthal, 1984; Bennis and Nanus, 1985; Hogan and Hogan, 1991 and Kaplan 1993).

IMPLICATIONS:

Use of speech and hearing behavior as presently conceived allows for a new approach to study of personality of executives, management and employees. Variations in speech and hearing, as explained in this theory and utilized in the study of executives, do not appear in DSM-IV as criteria for the making of any Axis I or Axis II psychiatric diagnosis nor would they be sufficient to qualify for disability benefits from the Social Security Administration. Rather, they appear to reflect variations in normal psychological functioning, which can be discerned in various areas of life.

What is a "normal" personality for one organization may not be true for another organization. Variation in acceptable personality traits may even vary within organizations depending on the work task. This protocol allows for easy collection of data to define individual work situations.

The protocol advocated in this report has the virtue of being brief (taking 5-10 minutes) and utilizing non-threatening stimuli (speech and hearing stimuli). It can be used with persons age three years and beyond and is racially, culturally and educationally non-discriminatory. Speech dialects are factored out in the interpretation of the findings. With the increasing sophistication of methods for voice and speech recognition, it may be possible to automate the data collection described in this paper. Until then, persons using this approach will need to depend on the identification skills of speech pathologists or take training in this area themselves. The integration of the meanings of speech and hearing data is likely to remain in the hands of psychologists.

Because of the ease of administration it can be used to collect descriptive data useful for team building as well as executive and employee selection. Validation studies utilizing the technique described in this paper should be completed in each instance in which this technique is employed. The approach presented in this paper offers a psychoanalytic model for understanding the personality of executives, managers, supervisors and technicians.

Integration of this approach with the current interest in the Five Factor Model, Jaques and Carson's concepts or any of the other past approaches to executive selection as summarized in Clark and Clark (1988) opens up new possibilities in cross theoretical study of personality functioning in organizations. Prospective studies using the present technique or any of the others noted above should have a high priority within organizations. The present author agrees with Hogan, Hogan and Robert's (1996) position that personality tests should only be one part of the decision to hire with past experiences, skill and training being of significant importance.

REFERENCES

Baehr, M. (1992). *Predicting Success in Higher-level Positions*. New York: Quorum Books.

Bennis, W. & Nanus, B. (1985). *Leaders*. New York: Harper.

Bradford, L. (1961). *Psychological Implications of the Strident "s"*. Unpublished undergraduate research project. Humboldt State University, Arcata, California.

Brende, J and Rinsley, D. (1979). Borderline disorder, altered states of consciousness and glossolalia. *J. American Academy of Psychoanalysis*, Vol 7,#2, 165-188.

Cantwell, D., Baker, L. & Mattison, R. (1979). The prevalence of psychiatric disorder in children with speech and language disorder. *J. Am. Academy of Child Psychiatry*, 450-461.

Chroniak, C. (1996). *Differentiating Between Successful and Unsuccessful Executives: A Psychodynamic Approach*. Ph.D. Dissertation, Loyola University, Chicago.

Clark, K. and Clark, M. (1988). *Measures of Leadership*. Leadership Library of America, Inc. West Orange, NJ.

Clark, L., Vorhies, L. & McEwen, J. (1994). Personality disorder symptomatology from the five factor model Perspective. In: Costa, P. & Widiger, T. (Eds.) *Personality Disorders and the Five Factor Model of Personality*, 95-116. American Psychological Association, Washington, DC.

Cozad, R. and Rousey, C. (1966). Hearing and speech disorders among delinquent children. *Corrective Psychiatry and Jrl. of Social Therapy.*, 12, 250-257.

DeVries, D. L. (1992). Executive selection: advances but no progress. *Issues and Observations,* 12, 1-5.

Fagundes, J. (1974). *A Study on Training Groups with Student Nurses.* Graduation Paper, Menninger School of Psychiatry.

Filippi, R. & Rousey, C. (1971). Positive carriers of violence among children: detection by speech deviations. *Mental Hygiene*, 55(2): 157-161.

Fleming, P. and Rousey, C. (1974). Quantification of psychotherapy change by study of speech and hearing patterns, 196-210. In: Rousey, C. (Ed.), *Psychiatric*

Assessment by Speech and Hearing Behavior. Charles C. Thomas, Springfield, IL., 1974.

Freud, A. (1946). *Ego and Mechanisms of Defense*. International Universities Press, NY, NY

Hogan, R., Hogan, J. and Roberts, B. (1996). Personality measurement and employment decisions, 469-477. *American Psychologist,* Vol 51, # 5.

Hogan, R., Raskin, R., & Frazzini, D. (1990). The dark side of charisma. In: K.E. Clark and M.B. Clark (Eds). *Measures of Leadership,* 343-354. West Orange, NJ: Leadership Library of America.

Hogan, R., Curphy, G. & Hogan, J. (1994). What we know about leadership. *American Psychologist*, Vol 49, #6, 493-504.

Irwin, O. (1947). Infant speech: consonantal sounds according to place of articulation. *Journal of Speech and Hearing Disorders*, 12, 397-401.

Irwin, O. (1948). Infant speech: Development of vowel sounds. *Journal of Speech and Hearing Disorders*, 13, 31-34.

Jaques, E. and Cason, K. (1994). *Human Capability*, Cason Hall & Company, Falls Church, Va.

Kaplan, R.E. (1993). The person behind the leader. *Executive Development*, 6,24-25.

Kernberg, O. (1979). Regression in organizational leadership. *Psychiatry*, 42, 24-39.

Kernberg, P. & Rousey, C. (1970). Variations in Speech Sounds During Psychotherapy. *American Academy of Child Psychiatry*, 9(4), 762-777.

LaFon, D. & Rousey, C. (1970). Residues of early-father child conflict. *Journal of Nervous and Mental Diseases,* 150(5), 366-370, 1970.

Levinson, H. (1980). Criteria for choosing chief executives. *Harvard Business Review*, #4, Vol. 58, 113-120

Levinson, H. (1994). Why the behemoths fell. *American Psychologist,* ,Vol 49, #5, 428-436.

Levinson H. and Rosenthal, S. (1984). *CEO*, Basic Books, Inc., NY.

Levy N. (1974). Aspects of speech pathology and psychoanalysis for the educator. In: C. Rousey, (Ed.)

Psychiatric Assessment by Speech and Hearing Behavior. Charles C. Thomas, Springfield, IL.

McDonald, E. (1964). *Articulation Testing and Treatment: A sensory-motor approach.* Pittsburgh, *Stanwix House.*

McDowell, R. (1968). *The Incidence of Speech Disorders among Emotionally Disturbed Children, Theoretical Implications: A reality approach to therapy,* ED.D. Thesis, University of Kansas.

Mehrhof, E. & Rousey, C. (1971). Speech difficulties symptomatic of destructive behavior toward self or others. *Journal of Nervous and Mental Hygiene,* 152(1): 63-67.

Norris, V. (1974). Speech Disturbances and the assessment of mental retardation in children. In: C. Rousey, Ed., *Psychiatric Assessment by Speech and Hearing Behavior,* Charles C. Thomas, Springfield, IL. 211-227.

Rousey, C. (1970). *Selection of Armed Forces Personnel.* Unpublished pilot study.

Rousey, C. (1971.) *Slips of the Tongue Revisited.* Unpublished graduation paper, Topeka Institute for Psychoanalysis.

Rousey, C. (1972). *Stability of Employment in an Industrial Complex*. Unpublished Pilot Study.

Rousey, C. (1973) *A Study of Factors Affecting Secretarial Employment*. Unpublished Pilot Study.

Rousey, C. (1974a). Use of the theory and procedures in psychiatric diagnosis. In: C. Rousey,(Ed.) *Psychiatric Assessment by Speech and Hearing Behavior*, 55-169. Charles C. Thomas, Springfield, IL.

Rousey, C. (1974b). A New Method to Select Psychiatric Residents. In: C. Rousey,(Ed.) *Psychiatric Assessment by Speech and Hearing Behavior,* 350-354. Charles C. Thomas, Springfield, IL.

Rousey, C. (1997). Normal and disturbed speech development. In: *The Handbook of Child and Adolescent Psychiatry, Vol II*. Joseph Noshpitz, Ed. in Chief, 436-443, John Wiley & Sons, NY, NY.

Rousey, C. and Averill, S. (1963). Speech disorders among delinquent boys. *Bulletin of the Menninger Clinic,* 177-184.

Rousey, C. and Mitchell, K. (1974). Selection of applicants for pastoral care training. In: C. Rousey,(Ed.) *Psychiatric Assessment by Speech and Hearing Behavior*, 355-366.

Rousey, C. and Moriarty, A. (1965). *Diagnostic Implications of Speech Sounds,* Charles C. Thomas, Springfield, IL.

Rousey C., Morrison, D. & Deacon, D. (1995). Choosing successful management, *Consulting Psychology Journal*, 47(2),108-113.

Rousey, C. and Rousey, W. (1995). *RAP (Rousey Assessment of Personality)-A Computerized Report.* Private Publication, Topeka, Kansas.

Sehdev, H. & Rousey, C. (1974). Speech deviation: indicator of underachievement. In: C. Rousey, (Ed.) *Psychiatric Assessment by Speech and Hearing Behavior,* 328-336, Charles C. Thomas, Springfield, IL.

Shriberg, L., Aram, D., Kwiatkowski, J. (1997). Developmental apraxia of speech: descriptive and theoretical perspectives. *JSLHR*, 40, (2), 273-285.

Stoel-Gammon, C. & Dunn, C. (1985). *Normal and Disordered Phonology in Children.* University Park Press, Baltimore.

Templin, M. (1957). *Certain Language Skills in Children.* The University of Minnesota Press, Minneapolis.

Tett. R., Jackson, D. and Rothstein, M. (1991). Personality measures as predictors of job performance: a meta-analytic review. *Personnel Psychology*, 44, 703-742.

Ware L. & Rousey, C. (1977). *Assessment of Change in a Therapeutic Nursery School.* Unpublished manuscript, Menninger Foundation.

Wells, J. (1972). *Incidence of articulation errors in orphans.* Unpublished undergraduate research project, Memphis State University.

Zaleznik, A. & Kets de Vries (1975). *Power and the Corporate Mind*, Boston: Hougton Mifflin.

Index